The Human Church

The Human Church

PAUL O. BISCHOFF

WIPF & STOCK · Eugene, Oregon

THE HUMAN CHURCH

Wipf & Stock
An Imprint of Wipf and Stock Publishers
199 W. 8th Ave., Suite 3
Eugene, OR 97401

www.wipfandstock.com

PAPERBACK ISBN: 978-1-5326-4233-3
HARDCOVER ISBN: 978-1-5326-4234-0
EBOOK ISBN: 978-1-5326-4235-7

Manufactured in the U.S.A.

To Matt who motivated me to write

Contents

Preface

THE HUMAN CHURCH, ROOTED in the biblical witness to the stories of God's people, takes anthropology for its trajectory. The Word did not become religion, God became flesh. Nor did humanity's Savior become a spirit. God became human. Jesus of Nazareth, a carpenter's son, whose mother was an unmarried teenager, was never called the second person of the Trinity in his Gospel biographies. Jesus' deity was consistently hidden as Luther's "beggar who walks the face of the earth incognito." The only beautiful woman, Mary from Magdala, in Grunewald's portrayal of Jesus' death, had a nonreligious reputation. The only theologian at the cross was a Roman centurion. Jesus loved Galilee's IRS employees more than the temple teachers. Jesus of Nazareth was the first authentic human being. The church who bears his name must be human if it's to have a spiritual impact on culture.

This book proposes a method for reading and interpreting Scripture presuming that good theology begins with good anthropology. The church is first a human community. Then it becomes a church. A feeding trough holds God in its straw; then it symbolizes the incarnation. Bread as bread, wine as wine, and cross as scandalous death tool only later become Eucharist and Christianity's ubiquitous symbol. A tomb as a final burial place is mysteriously emptied amid lies and cover-up and later becomes why the church says, "He is risen. He is risen indeed!"

Today's Christian community in America needs a human touch. The church needs to become more incarnational, not pious or religious. In one of his last letters, Dietrich Bonhoeffer encouraged the church to express biblical concepts in the vernacular of the day. *The Human Church* urges Christians to speak the gospel using a religion-less vocabulary with a human accent.

I wish to thank both Matthew Wimer, RaeAnne Harris, and Brian Palmer for their help, patience, and courtesy throughout the publication process. I'm grateful for Lee McCullough's theological insights and Grant Lantz's listening ear. My wife, Jayne, created the space of affirmation and encouragement readable in between the lines on every page.

October 29, 2017   Paul O. Bischoff
Reformation Sunday in its 500th Year
Wheaton

Introduction

THE CHURCH DOESN'T NEED to become more spiritual, but more incarnational, if it's to survive and flourish in the twenty-first century. It needs to become more human. The Apostle John offered the first-century church a test to detect whether "the spirit at your door" was the Spirit of God. "This is how you can recognize the Spirit of God: Every spirit that acknowledges that Jesus Christ has come in the flesh is from God."[1] The phrase "in the flesh" is key. It's another way to say that God became human. Given the "mystical buffet" of spiritual experiences available today, it's critical that we keep coming back to John's profound words.

During a long series of addresses from 1979 to 1984, John Paul II spoke about having an "adequate anthropology" to have a total vision of humanity. The pope stated that the body, and it alone, is capable of making visible what is invisible, the spiritual and divine. It was created to transfer into the visible reality of the world, the invisible mystery hidden in God. Both the Apostle John and Pope John Paul II have a countercultural approach for the church in its mission. As the culture becomes more "spiritual," the church needs to focus upon the physical body and its meaning from creation and the incarnation.

This book attempts to fulfill the pope's quest for such an "adequate anthropology." So let's start right up front with a disclaimer. I'm a theologian, not an anthropologist. I come to the study of anthropology as an outsider. I believe that starting with

1. 1 John 4:2.

anthropology provides a more robust theology. Actually, my theology of creation and incarnation creates space for doing anthropology in the church. Since God thought enough of humanity to create women and men in his image, being human must be important to the Creator. Since God became human so we could touch God, an anthropological method for finding meaning in the church must be worth considering.

When it came to proving his post-death identity, Jesus preferred anthropology to spirituality. In his first encounter with the disciples he showed them the puncture wounds on his hands and a large laceration on his side. Thomas believed only because he touched Jesus' unhealed wounds. Ironically, Jesus touched him. When on the Sea of Galilee and still unrecognized by his fishing followers, Jesus barbecued fish for breakfast. Once fed, Jesus then challenged Peter theologically to be a pastor in the church. Jesus' method was first anthropological, then theological. *The human church* begins with anthropology and ends with theology just like when Jesus healed a man's paralyzed legs and then forgave his sins.

That said, historic roadblocks exist for doing anthropological-theology study. "To a great extent, anthropology first defined itself as a rational, empirically-based enterprise quite different from theology. The theology it repudiated was, for the most part, Christian."[2] Author Fenella Carnell rethinks the past conflict between anthropology and Christianity anticipating a more collaborative relationship between science and church. Tim Larsen, in a more recent study, affirms Carnell's vision. During research among household anthropologists, he discovered that many anthropologists had church affiliations: Mary Douglas (devout Catholic), Margaret Mead (active Episcopalian), Victor Turner (convert from Marxism to Catholicism) and E. E. Evans-Pritchard (adult convert to Catholicism).[3] He, too, sees a way to solve the riddle between anthropology and the church.

Yet the desire to incorporate anthropological methods within mission is not new. In 1929 Darrell L. Whiteman mentioned that

2. Cannell, *Anthropology of Christianity*, 14.

3. Larsen, *Slain God*, 7.

it was Malinowski who called for anthropology "to move beyond the sterile confines of academia and enter the world where cultures were clashing with one another."[4] In his substantive article, Whiteman opines, "Why are so many missionaries, Protestant and Catholic, Western and non-Western, unaware of the value of anthropology for their work and ministry?" His argument draws on the incarnation which "shows us that God has taken both humanity and culture seriously."[5]

Dietrich Bonhoeffer's theology was informed more than anything else by the bodily suffering the Jews endured by the Nazis. I believe his anthropological approach sets the stage for his robust and radical theology. He spoke of a way of knowing "from below," from the perspective of the outcasts, the suspects, the maltreated, the powerless, the oppressed and reviled, in short from the perspective of the suffering."[6] A common thread in the above points out how theology is enriched by anthropology. We proceed with our study within the context of Jesus' approach to people and from the impact on Bonhoeffer's view of the Jews' suffering. The following analysis of Christian rituals and symbols seen from the ordinary is my attempt to provide a segment of "adequate anthropology" so that the church may become less spiritual and more incarnational; that is, more human.

Structurally, the book is divided into two parts: part 1: Anthropology, and part 2: Theology. Part 1 (chapters 1 through 4) provides an overview of the human behavior involving the symbols observed in communal rituals. Part 2 (chapters 5 through 8) interprets Christianity's symbols theologically. To begin, the reader is put into the position of an ethnographer recording observed human behavior, to get the "feel" of an anthropological study of a people group. The people group in this book is the human community called the church. Observed behavior during its rituals is where we begin. Chapter 1, "Human Beings in Community," sets the stage for how the reader will "see and hear" worship during

4. Whiteman, "Part II: Anthropology and Mission," 21.

5. Ibid.

6. Bonhoeffer, *Letters and Papers from Prison*, 52.

certain seasons of the church calendar. Part 1 makes no claim at interpreting what is seen and heard during the rituals; that's for part 2 where questions raised by anthropology are addressed theologically. To elevate the different objectives for part 1 and 2, references to texts in part 1 will simply state the book and page number appearing, for example as, "New International Version Study Bible, 1546." In part 2, the same text would appear using the actual name given in the Bible with chapter and verse, without a page number; e.g., "John 3:16." Because of the many texts used in part 2, general reference to only the Gospels or Epistles may be used when citing several texts for the sake of readability.

Chapters 2, 3, and 4 focus upon the observed and narrative behaviors pertinent to a manger, bread, wine, cross, and tomb, respectively. "Observed behavior" is what the reader actually sees during community rituals. "Narrative behavior" is what the reader "sees" in the behaviors of persons in texts read during the ritual. Correlations between observed and narrative behaviors are particularly important to our study. The "texts" are taken from the sacred literature referred to as the Bible or the biblical witness. The rituals and symbols are gleaned from Christianity's sacred literature spanning a history of two thousand years before and one hundred years after the birth of Jesus called the Old and New Testaments.

The primary objective of part 2: Theology, is to interpret the ethnographic data from part 1 using religion-less language. Certain concepts and traditional terms correspond to the rituals and symbols from part 1. Historically, these concepts and terms have been academic, not ordinary. Part 2 seeks to address the issue of language attempting to put lofty ideas and abstract terms into accessible language without loss of meaning. This objective of putting biblical concepts into "nonreligious language" originates with Dietrich Bonhoeffer, our conversation partner throughout part 2. Bonhoeffer will guide our theological discussion of the church, the incarnation, redemption, and the resurrection.

The chapters in part 1 parallel the chapters in part 2. That is, chapter 1 and chapter 5 relate; here the anthropology of a human community is interpreted as the theology of the church. Chapters

2 and 6 correspond in that a feeding trough called a manger is theologically discussed as the incarnation. Chapters 3 and 7 link bread, wine, and a cross to redemption, followed by chapters 4 and 8 where a tomb and resurrection go together.

Prior to beginning, we need to clarify the word "liturgy." Liturgy is a misunderstood word in the church today. Too often it is confined to the Sunday worship service. Literally, liturgy is the "work of the people." This definition has critical implications for the church. The church is a human community which gathers and scatters. The gathered church meets on Sunday for celebration to ascribe "worthship" to God; but liturgy doesn't end with the benediction. The scattered church disperses through the week to obey Christ's commands in lifestyle and service. Both behaviors are liturgical; that is, the church is always worshiping God.

As anthropologists, we will view the church as an ethnographic object. The anthropological categories employed during ethnographic analysis include origin/history, distribution, physical/material traits, social groupings, racial/ethnic groupings, behavioral variables, and integrated patterns of knowledge, belief, and behavior.[7] The category "integrated patterns of knowledge, belief, and behavior" is particularly important.

Finally, a word about how this book views ritual and symbol. Ritual is a repeated event involving communal human behavior. For example, the first ritual studied is the lighting of the Advent wreath. Throughout the church, in some form or another, this ritual is practiced during Advent. Symbol, on the other hand, doesn't involve observable behavior even though it may appear in a ritual. A symbol is a commonly recognized token of identity. So for the church, a manger symbolizes Advent/Christmas. While no communal behavior is associated with the manger, it is more than just a sign of Christ's birth. As a symbol it brings together both a material feeding trough and its spiritual meaning as the unlikely place of God's birth. Anthropologically, we'll speak of the manger in its own right culturally. Then, we'll get into the manger's theological importance for the incarnation. We'll be careful to observe

7. Whitehead, "Basic Classical Ethnographic Research Methods," 41.

how an anthropological view of the manger enriches our grasp of the mysterious God-human who makes it his crib. The manger is not an end in itself but it "participates in the reality" of the incarnation.[8] The next chapter launches our anthropological analysis of a human community as it gathers for its Sunday worship service.

8. Vander Zee, *Christ, Baptism and the Lord's Supper*, 33.

Part One

Anthropology

Chapter 1

Human Beings in Community

IN THIS CHAPTER WE observe a community of human beings gathered for Sunday worship. You are the ethnographer observing and documenting what you see and hear related to the behavior of the community. You are not a participant as you are used to being. You are challenged now to assume that you've never been to such a ritual for this people group. You have no interest in the quality of the worship or your feelings about anything you observe other than to jot notes or questions. Your feelings do not constitute data in our anthropological study. As mentioned, in chapter 5 we will call this people group a church. There, and not before, we will interpret and offer meaning to the data you record during this chapter.

We will be sensitive to two types of human behavior: observed and narrative. You will actually see the observed behavior. You will "see" the behavior of persons in texts from the Bible which are read during the ritual. Taken together, both types offer a robust perspective.

Several mini-rituals occur during the overall ritual of this people group's worship. These are documented in what's called the bulletin or order of service. The worshipers call this the liturgy of the ritual. Along with the liturgy you will notice tokens or artifacts which seem to be important since they are seen in different places, mentioned in readings or sung about by the people. The symbols, as we will call them, identify the people group. For example, you've seen a vertical-horizontal arrangement of material (wood or metal) where the vertical portion is longer than the horizontal. This symbol appears at the top of the building on a steeple, on the front wall of the sanctuary, on a table, in print in the bulletin and virtually everywhere. Of course, this is a cross. So let's begin by going through the ritual of worship. You will have lots of questions about origin and history. Unfortunately, very few answers come from observing human behavior. So there's a lot of behind-the-scenes research involved in finding out more about what you see and hear. We'll assume that you've been to enough services to be familiar with worship styles, people arrangements, building use, etc. From time to time, we'll speak as if you've never been to a worship service.

As you enter the building, someone greets you and hands you a bulletin. Another person shows you to a seat on a long wooden bench in the balcony. You've been to other similar people groups where individual chairs are used. You arrive ten minutes early and hear an organ, piano, or instrumental music by musicians or electronically over a sound system. You look around a lot during this time. We begin our analysis by applying certain categories to this gathering of a human community in worship.

Categories of Anthropological Analysis[1]

Physical/Material Characteristics

This category of anthropological analysis is comprehensive and attempts to describe everything about the tangible layout, lighting, temperature, musical instruments, decor, symmetry and balance, flooring, furniture, colors, art and symbols in the room which the people group calls a sanctuary. Your seat from the balcony offers a good view. Your attention is drawn to the windows; they contain colorful art with persons and symbols which are different in each one. You make a note: Who are these people? What is this art communicating about the people group? You've been in other

---

1. Whitehead, "Basic Classical Ethnological Research Methods," 27–43.

buildings where the windows are plain; so you have questions about the importance of colored windows compared to plain ones.

The very front of the room is complicated and varied in its decor, furniture, musical instrumentation, and floral displays. A large wooden cross is on the back wall. In front of it is a screen used to display art, messages, biblical texts, and words for songs. On the far right side there is a lectern which is quite a bit larger than most you've seen in classrooms or other meeting halls. In the center, there is a table with a book and a cross flanked by two candles on either end. Over to the left side there is an arrangement of musical instruments. An organ rests on the back of a platform which is accessible from a wide set of three stairs from the front and three stairs from the right side. On the floor level there is a piano on the left side near the other musical instruments. Below the lectern (the people group calls this a pulpit) there is a piece of furniture unique to this sacred space which contains water. You're told this is a baptismal font; you make a note to question its use and significance. For added seating two alcoves exist to the left and the right with cushioned chairs facing the platform at an angle. Wall art appears in the form of framed pictures and posters. Banners are displayed from the ceiling on both sides of the room near entrances to both alcoves.

Beyond the large sacred space there is a narrow space called a narthex or lobby, which is the first space one enters from the front door of the building. You've noticed that few people come in by the front door of the church into the narthex and that few leave through that entrance. As you see people arriving about three minutes before the service is scheduled to start, you notice that most are entering the room through a set of doors to the front of the sanctuary and make their own way to a seat having been greeted by someone at the doors. You make of note of this. At the conclusion of the service, another space is used for a coffee hour in closer proximity to an entrance right off the parking lot.

People Group Characteristics & Race-Ethnic-Class Variables

As people begin to gather you notice that they are predominately white middle-class persons with a few African Americans, Africans, Asian Americans, and many children of Asian descent. Over several weeks and months you've noticed that people generally sit in the same places. The number of worshipers on average is about two hundred. Many are dressed casually; you learn that they are professionals, many of whom commute by train into the city. Some walk into the service with coffee purchased on the outside. You recognize this as an ordinary cultural behavior and may wonder if it has any place in the liturgy.

The dominant social grouping would be families with several widows and widowers, graduate, undergraduate, and high school students who sit in the same place every Sunday with their youth pastor. The service is comprised of several young children who are given special attention and recognition. There is a multigenerational flavor to the congregation where most adults range in the forties to eighties category with a few families in their twenties and thirties.

Classification

Classification can go many different directions in an anthropological study. For our purposes, it makes most sense to adhere to "a punctuation of time through significant ritual events." As far as the church is concerned this would follow how the church segments time according to its seasons, beginning with Advent, Christmas, Epiphany, Lent, and Holy Week, which includes Maundy Thursday, Good Friday, the Easter Vigil, and Easter. Beyond Easter, church observance becomes flexible and may or may not include special observance of Ascension Sunday, Pentecost, or Trinity Sunday. There is the elongated period of so-called Ordinary Time. With varying degrees these seasons of the church calendar are explained by the pastor or in the bulletin. During Lent many churches add extra periods of contemplation and meditation to regular Sunday worship.

Specific to our study will be the seasons of Advent/Christmas, Lent, Holy Week, and Easter. For each of these seasons we will perform an informal ethnographic study of a key ritual and symbol which characterize the worship.

Behavioral Variables

Common rituals may exist outside the special seasons of the church year. For example, all gatherings of the people group for worship include singing. The words may be from a book called the hymnal or from the screen. The community typically stands to sing; although they sing while sitting as well. The songs may be quiet, contemplative or joyous and vigorous. During the singing, some people hold up their hands. You also observe people on the platform who lead singing along with a band of instruments including guitars, keyboard, drums, and on special occasions a cello, flute, or other orchestral instruments. Along with the congregational singing, a choir sings once or twice during a service. This may be at the very beginning or during a time when plates are passed to collect money for the church, called the offering. Certain songs are sung at certain points of every service. For example, the same song, called a Doxology, is sung after the offering. The community sings a song with everyone holding hands right after the pastor concludes the worship with a final prayer, called the benediction.

There are times when the entire community is silent with their eyes closed. This often occurs when the pastor says, "Please join me in prayer or let us pray together." You make a special note of prayer as a ritual. The behavior you observe is passive. People have their eyes closed and you discover that they believe they are communicating with God. Anthropologically, this is problematic since one can't really observe prayer. More on this situation in our theological analysis.

Essentially, the observed behaviors of the pastor and worship leaders include speaking, reading, singing, and praying. The major behaviors for the people include listening, reading, reciting, praying, taking notes during a sermon, and singing. Often the congregation is asked to stand and recite/read what is called a creed, or a statement of belief. You observe that many can do this without looking at the words in the bulletin or on the screen. Musicians play their respective instruments to accompany congregational singing. Both the piano and the organ are played together or individually either at the beginning or at the end of the service.

Special mention needs to be given to the observed behavior of the pastor called preaching. You notice that even though this involves a specific text from the Bible, it is more than reading. Also, even though knowledge is dispensed during the sermon, it is more than teaching. There is a unique quality to this preaching. No matter the church season, preaching always occurs toward the middle of the service. The sermon may last from fifteen to thirty-five minutes. It is characterized by emotion, challenge, conviction, instruction, interpretation of a text, and application for daily living. At times the pastor requests prayer before the sermon and may also invite the congregation to pray for themselves so they "may hear the voice of God." While there is no audible voice heard during the sermon other than the pastor's, people often remark how God spoke to them during the sermon. Of course, this is difficult to record as observed data.

As stated above, certain rituals are repeated during seasons of the church calendar, and others appear during all worship services. During what is called Communion the community eats bread and drinks wine/juice. Baptism involves water; for an infant, by sprinkling water from the font on its head up front while parents and others stand with the pastor. The pastor baptizes while reciting the words, "In the name of the Father, the Son and the Holy Spirit." Another form of baptism is called immersion, which typically occurs for adults and involves both pastor and parishioner standing in water up to their waist. The pastor puts the person under water and quickly pulls them up. Baptism occurs in a specially designed tank in the front of the sanctuary. The ritual of baptism may occur anytime; unlike other rituals, it is neither regularly repeated nor bound by the church calendar.

Finally, you observe that behavior is directed by the bulletin or is spontaneous by pastor, leaders, or people during the worship;

that is, the pastor may pray at points not indicated in the bulletin. At times, the congregation is given space during prayer to audibly voice their personal prayers. There is nothing in the bulletin which prescribes this behavior. You've been told that this is "Spirit-led."

The above is a snapshot of the observed behaviors typical of the worship of this community; it is not exhaustive. In the chapters to follow, where specific rituals and symbols are discussed, you will see many of these behaviors repeated. We now consider how the community may be anthropologically assessed as to its social groupings.

Social Groupings

Viewing this people group in its largest gathering in celebration doesn't include smaller social groupings which characterize the community. However, you do notice in the bulletin a variety of men's and women's groups for prayer and study. Other social groupings include an activity program for young people of middle and high school age. So you decide to attend one of the groups: the choir rehearsal. Along with the practice for the Sunday's anthem, you observe a community spirit within the group. One choir member likened it to a "church within the church." Often, there is a brief time of prayer requests. Your overall sense of social groupings is that those who participate feel it's a significant activity which keeps them in the church. Many people you interview speak of their small group as that place where their friendships are formed and where they feel a sense of intimacy. Some compare their small group to the conversation during coffee hour after the service. While connections are made with people you need to see, many prefer the authenticity of relationships among members of their small group, choir, or other more intimate social groupings in the community.

Classes, prayer groups, and study groups, as you discover through individual interviews, seem to be mini-versions of the large worship service. That is, elements of the group derive from the worship service: reading, prayer, hearing, teaching, and study. The participation is more active than in the worship service. With fewer people, more interaction can occur to answer questions.

Many feel their small group study during the week complements the preaching heard on Sundays. The leadership team, itself an important small group elected by the church, has worked with the pastor to implement a common theme for both small group study and Sunday service sermons. The idea of commonality raises a critical question: Given so diverse a human community, what is the common denominator which draws and holds these people together? While an anthropological study observes and records data, it may not reveal an answer to this question. In fact, this people group appears to defy such an answer. The group spans gender, age, socioeconomic, and class data. We table further discussion on this issue, since we'll show later that the uniqueness of this people group is the invisibility of its common thread. In sum, no observable common denominator for this people group exists; thus, the need for theological interpretation.

Integrated Patterns of Knowledge, Belief, and Behavior

The most important category for our analysis is *integrated patterns of knowledge, belief, and behavior*. In a way this category summarizes much of what we learn separately from previous categories. Taken separately we know the community hears knowledge from what is read, taught, and preached as texts from the Bible. As already mentioned, the texts are historic events or stories illustrating behavior conveying an important teaching. We've called this narrative behavior. Rabbi Jesus used parables throughout his life to convey his teaching. Often the teaching involves the behaviors by which one who is faithful should live. So we begin with specifying the importance of narrative behavior from sacred texts which may mandate acceptable behaviors observable outside the text.

Along with behavior to be modeled by persons in the texts, the sacred literature contains tenets of belief stated as assertions, claims, or truth statements. These statements tend to be conceptual and abstract, while narrative behaviors are specific and concrete.

Adding in the observed behavior of persons during a worship service, we begin to get a model of integration, which involves *knowledge* from the sacred texts and statements of *belief*, which together influence the desired faithful *behavior* of the community. For example, anthropologically we can determine that certain behaviors have occurred during the worship because historic sacred texts have spoken of a similar people group who did so. Because it was modeled in the sacred text, the community heard it preached by its pastor during sermons. If the pastor thought it was important enough to be proclaimed, the community understands that both beliefs and behaviors are important enough to be trusted and performed.

So a pattern of knowledge, belief, and behavior develops through the repetition of worship, prayer, study, and small groups. Over time the integration of knowledge, belief, and behavior emerges as a culture unique to the people group. It is defined by its culture. In fact, individual members of the people group are so imbued with the culture that they don't even have to think about what or why they behave as they do. The people group understands how knowledge, belief, and behavior are integrated within its community life. That is, parishioners realize that when aberrant behavior occurs, it is called out for the protection of the community. The cohesion of the community appears to be a function of beliefs beyond the scope of this chapter, more appropriately addressed in part 2.

Conclusion

The intent of this chapter was to launch your task as an ethnographer; that is, as a recorder of observed human behavior to which we've added narrative behavior from the sacred texts of the people group. This chapter sets the stage for an anthropology of key rituals and symbols. We've also established certain categories of analysis for our study.

We begin our study in the next chapter by focusing on the ritual of lighting the Advent wreath, accompanied by a manger as its symbol.

Chapter 2

A Manger

IN THE PREVIOUS CHAPTER we assumed the role of anthropologists within a community of worshiping human beings. In this chapter we'll focus upon a ritual of lighting the Advent wreath and its associated symbol, the manger, celebrated during the season of Advent. Throughout the discussion, as it will always be in part 1: Anthropology, our objective is to take note of what we see and hear relative to both ritual and symbol using ethnographic categories. Lighting an Advent wreath and a manger suggest particular attention to the following categories: Overall physical variables, origin and history, behavioral variables, social groupings, and integrated patterns of knowledge, belief, and behavior. All references to sacred texts are taken from the biographies of Jesus written by his followers. The community calls these the Gospels.

An Ethnography of Lighting the Advent Wreath

Overall Physical Variables

Looking around the sanctuary we observe that in one week the room has gone from the fruits and vegetables of harvest celebrated at Thanksgiving to "everything red and green." There's a pine tree, a Christmas tree you've seen virtually everywhere during this time of year, off to one side of the platform. On the other side of the platform, hanging from a long wire, is a horizontal wreath with different colored candles spaced evenly around it with a taller white candle in the middle. It's called an Advent wreath. There are other more traditional wreaths hanging from every window with globed candles on the window sills. You look around to notice a long string of garland across the balcony. You also observe the color purple on decorative cloths on the pulpit and also worn by the pastor. On a table, there is a curious display of figurines in a stable with animals. It visualizes readings you've heard about Mary, Joseph, and baby Jesus in a manger (a feeding trough for the animals). Upon a closer look, you notice that the manger is empty. An explanation of these figurines in the bulletin calls this a nativity scene. The sanctuary reflects the season of the church calendar called Advent. What's Advent?

Origin & History

No one really knows when *Advent* was introduced into the church community in conjunction with the birth of Jesus of Nazareth, although secret celebrations of his birth occurred in the second century. It wasn't until the sixth century that Advent publicly ritualized the baby born in Bethlehem, since Constantine established Christianity as a legal religion in the Roman Empire. The season of Advent is practiced during the four Sundays before Christmas. Advent is a time of preparation and waiting for Jesus' actual birth. The Christian calendar begins on the first Sunday of Advent, so it's even possible to say "Happy New Year" to one another, along with "Merry Christmas." Given a brief background of Advent, we now turn our attention to the ritual lighting of the Advent wreath and then the manger as the key symbol of Advent/Christmas.

By definition a wreath is a circular arrangement of flowers, twigs, leaves, or various materials. The Advent wreath is a garland of evergreen branches that goes back to the fifth century BC, when it would have been worn as a crown. Laurel wreaths were worn by the Greeks and Romans to symbolize rank or achievement; thus, the wearing of wreaths by victorious athletes at the original

Olympic Games. Prior to Christianity, Northern European tribes practiced a ritual of welcoming spring with a circular wreath of evergreens, where candles symbolized the arrival of increased light coming out of winter. So, Christianity actually accommodated a pagan ritual into its worship, where the theme of light meant something totally different from the common cultural understanding. In Christianity, Advent wreaths adorn sanctuaries on the first Sunday of Advent. German Lutherans first used Advent wreaths in the sixteenth century. Later, in the nineteenth century a cartwheel with evergreen branches gave rise to the modern version we observe today as earlier observed, the wreath is horizontal and may hang from a long wire attached to the room ceiling or lay flat on a table with four candles on its periphery and one taller white candle at the center. Given a closer look, you see that three candles on the circle are purple and one is pink.

Behavioral Variables: Ritual and Symbol

At the beginning of the service, after an opening prayer, there is a period of silence when from the rear of the auditorium people slowly walk to light one of the candles, after which one person reads a portion of the Bible. The reading for the first Sunday of Advent goes with a purple candle, called the prophecy candle, because it symbolizes how the prophets foretold the birth of a baby. You hear a reading from the Prophet Isaiah. The second Advent candle, also purple, is often called the Bethlehem candle, speaking of the manger as the baby's humble crib. The third candle is rose-colored or pink and typically represents the joy the shepherds felt as they arrived at the manger. Finally, the fourth candle, purple, represents peace and is often called the Angels' candle. The taller white candle remains unlit. Of all the candles, only the second one symbolizes a tangible object, the manger.

You observe creative methods of doing the readings. In some cases, only one reading occurs per candle. Other approaches may include a reading with a prayer or the lighting and one person sharing a spiritual experience associated with the theme for each candle. At times the congregation responds with a reading or song.

Each approach introduces the candle in its own way. The Advent wreath indicates how the manger is *the* primary symbol both for Advent and Christmas. The birth of Jesus in a manger marks the historical beginning of those who believe that the baby was the king of the Jews. This is why Advent is the first season of the calendar. The lighting of the white candle, taller than all others, typically occurs in a midnight Christmas Eve service, the most important event during Advent prior to Christmas, the birthday of the baby. The Advent wreath prepares the way for the manger to which we now turn our attention.

An Ethnography of the Manger

Origin & History

We notice that the manger appears in the nativity scene. Yet the nativity scene may or may not be in the sanctuary. It may appear in what's called a living crèche, where human beings, including a real baby, inhabit a wooden stable constructed on the lawn close enough to the street that passersby may see it. We note that there is no ritual for the manger, per se. That is, there is no specific observable behavior which corresponds to the manger in the same way it does for the Advent wreath.

As for origin, the manger goes back at least to the first century according to the biblical data related to the birth of Jesus of Nazareth. There is no precedent in any other culture where a manger is used for the crib of an infant. This use of a manger is unique. It's unique in history, not merely church history. Its meaning is uniquely mysterious in its own right. That a feeding trough was used by human beings in this first-century culture as a baby crib is unheard of, not to mention unsanitary!

There is widespread confusion over how to translate "inn." To discuss this involves a bit of textual analysis. Traditionally, the word *inn* is erroneously contextualized as, say, a Holiday Inn. A mythical "innkeeper" is said to point Mary and Joseph to a cave or a stable. Most nativity scenes use a stable with a wooden feeding trough. But "inn" is best translated "guest room in a house." If so, a manger is not a wooden crib, but an indentation in either a limestone wall or in the ground floor of a house where animals are sheltered from the cold. The manger is filled with food for oxen, cows, or sheep; probably straw. There was no room in the second-floor guest room, so they settled on the ground floor stable. In sum, no cultural depiction of an "inn" as a motel or a manger as a wooden crib exists in the first century.

The etymology of "*manger*" suggests an integration of knowledge, belief, and behavior. It is derived from the French verb "to eat." In Italian, to eat is encouraged with "*mangia, mangia*."[1] Further, the part of our jaw which assists in chewing is called a *mandible*. So this baby spends his first moments on earth in a device which offers food for the hungry. Consistent with a theme of eating and food, the little town of Bethlehem is best translated "house of bread." So Jesus of Nazareth is born in a town named for bread in a device to feed animals.

Social Groupings

The social groupings at the manger include, of course, the parents with their baby and shepherds, who have been supernaturally told to find the manger. We refer to textual evidence which indicates that the shepherds saw and heard what the biblical witness refers to as angels. Whether others observed/heard this communication, the reader is never told. We only know that shepherds went to the manger to validate what they had heard. From the narrative behavior we observe only a family and shepherds at the manger. The varied social groups involved in Jesus' birth include a poor, young Jewish family; low-income Jewish workers at the bottom of the social scale whose job it was to maintain enough sheep for religious sacrifices. Ironically, a biblical birth narrative including

1. *Merriam-Webster*, s.v. "manger."

low-class worshiping shepherds indicates a prophecy that a ruler of the Jews will be a shepherd of Israel. So we have a diversity of class distinctions associated with visits to Jesus at his birth. Persian astrologers later visited the young Jesus, now a toddler living with his parents in a house.

The biblical witness states that the shepherds would have two signs to go on to be sure of the infant's identity: (1) he'd be in a manger; (2) he'd be wrapped in swaddling cloths. By definition, swaddling clothes/cloths are strips of cloth wrapped around a new-born child to hold its legs and arms still so the infant doesn't harm itself.[2] This would have made perfect sense in a manger with the sharp ends of straw as a mattress. The word connotes restraint of action and a limiting of movement for one's protection and safety. The key in both the manger and the cloths wrapped around Jesus' body is that here we have a unique sign that the shepherds weren't at the bedside of just any baby in Bethlehem that night, but near the infant about which they had been told. From this brief analysis of social groups associated with the manger, we can now turn our attention to how the textual narrative of the story offers knowledge about the behaviors of Mary and Joseph. The next section attempts to locate patterns which integrate knowledge, belief, and behaviors related to Advent's ritual and symbol.

Integrated Patterns of Knowledge, Belief, and Behavior

The five candles in the Advent wreath all point to the manger as the key symbol for Advent/Christmas. Three colored candles comprise the wreath—purple, pink, and white. Its lighting prompts readings of the narratives related to the manger. Its practice also involves a diversity of persons: singles, young and old, and families. Those persons who celebrate the ritual emulate the diversity of angels, shepherds, and a young family gathered around the infant. That is, a cross-section of society surrounds the feeding trough which

2. Duchesne, *Christian Worship*, 260.

contains this baby. More on this later as we discuss the diversity of the church in part 2.

Part of the value in viewing Jesus' birth anthropologically is that sentimental, nostalgic, and religious notions are removed. While we'll view the manger theologically later, looking through an ethnographic lens now enables us to see things as they really are without interpretation, piety, or religion. The countercultural placing of a baby in a manger suggests the word *scandal*. There aren't many Christmas carols devoted to the scandal of the manger! But viewing the manger anthropologically strips away the religion and ironically makes for better theology.

It's easy to miss the cultural scandal of the manger because the biblical evidence for Jesus' birth proceeds so matter-of-factly without commentary by the Gospel authors. Exactly what is it about the manger which makes the birth of Jesus scandalous?

Consider the actual events, conversations, and decisions related to Jesus' birth which precede the manger. The primary communication for Jesus' birth to those involved happens through angels and dreams. An angel tells a teenage girl that she will become pregnant by a spirit. Her husband-to-be wants to break off the wedding when she tells him she's pregnant. Then he's told in a dream about the supernatural biology of the baby's birth. They must now convey this information to their parents. To the extent that we fill in the blanks anthropologically where the biblical witness is silent, we humanize the story making it more credible and less religious. While the biblical evidence about scandal isn't explicit, we can infer it from the reactions of Mary and Joseph in their dialogue with the angels. Joseph thinks he needs to divorce Mary quietly. Mary's "How will this be?" is the key anthropological question regarding the conception of her baby. She's terrified by the greeting; even more by the message. She resolves her anxiety by recalling her relationship to God as his servant as she submits to the mysterious process of her baby's conception.

Acting as anthropologists, we're sensitive to how the birth narratives model an integrated pattern of knowledge, belief, and behavior. The message is highly theological. But Mary's thinking is anthropological. She's told that God favors her. She's not sure what that means. Then she's told her baby will be the son of a king with a never-ending reign. She might be tempted to start believing all this given the privilege, power, and recognition of being this child's mother. However, Mary isn't impressed. She's concerned about her body. Right after asking the human question "How will this be?" she's told that the spirit about to impregnate her is from Yahweh, the unspeakable God of Abraham, Isaac, and Jacob. Knowing this, Mary decides to cooperate with the process even though the answer to her question is mysterious. Her fear turns to trust. The message shifts from the unknown to the known. "For nothing is impossible with God." Mary's response goes from belief to behavior. "May it be to me as you have said," which is another way to say: "I don't understand how or why, but I'm ready to go through with this."

Admittedly, we're limited to non-observable narrative behavior within the sacred text. We haven't seen or heard Mary say these things. We have only the biblical witness of an author's interpretation of secondhand information. That said, there is another way to approach this anthropologically. It's an adaptation of "participant observation."[3] We "live" with Mary in the text. We recognize her humanity as our humanity. All teenage mothers know what Mary is going through. All mothers of teenage mothers know how they feel as Mary's mother may have felt. All boyfriends of teenage mothers understand Joseph's questions. We also feel the scandal because we see it all the time in our culture. To that end, we're observers. And the manger is what it is. At this point we view it as a unique symbol of the mysterious and scandalous birth of a baby-king.

While beyond the scope of observed behavior, we can't help but speculate on other methods which may have been used to introduce the king of the universe (Jesus of Nazareth) into humanity. Would not less scandal have accompanied the mysterious birth of a baby to a legally married couple? Why must this king come as a helpless infant; why not as a capable adult with powerful rhetoric, self-assurance, and confidence? Why not the military hero an

---

3. Whiteman, "Part II: Anthropology and Mission," 80.

occupied Jewish nation wanted? Anthropologically, it would have been far more logical to introduce Jesus as the savior of humanity, consistent with a Moses, David, or Joshua. More people might have believed. But here we border on theological interpretation.

Conclusion

To summarize, we've analyzed the lighting of the Advent wreath ritual and manger as the unique symbol for Advent/Christmas. We began our analysis by observing the behavior related to the ritual: lighting the Advent wreath. Focusing upon the integrated patterns of knowledge, belief, and behavior related to the manger, we observed Mary's movement from fear to faith despite the scandal of her baby's birth. In Mary, we see a courageous human being willing to cooperate with a mysterious process involving the conception of human life. She anticipates the integration of knowledge, belief, and behavior for all future followers of her baby, for she's given difficult information, struggles to believe it, and yet ultimately obeys an angel's message.

We now turn our attention to another significant ritual of our people group: The Eucharist and its accompanying symbols: bread, wine, and a cross.

Chapter 3

Bread, Wine, and a Cross

IN THE PREVIOUS CHAPTER we observed behaviors of a people group in its Advent/Christmas ritual of lighting the Advent wreath symbolized by a manger. In this chapter we perform an anthropological analysis of the ritual eating bread and drinking wine symbolized by a cross. We've selected certain categories to analyze the ritual and the symbol.

The Ethnography of Eating Bread and Drinking Wine

Origin, History & Narrative Behavior

The origin and history of eating bread and drinking wine as the ritual of Communion (also called Eucharist) has its roots in the life of the Jewish people as recorded in the Torah. In fact, the ritual originates from the last plague endured by Egypt. Of course, that history is Israel's as well since it was held captive in slavery by Egypt's leader, Pharaoh. We begin with a careful look at the narrative behavior involving the reluctance of Egypt to free the Jewish slaves.

The Torah records that an angel of death was to come over all of the country and kill the firstborn child and firstborn animal of every home. Jewish homes would be "passed over" by killing a lamb without defect, roasting and eating it hastily, and putting its blood on the top and two sides of their doorframes. When the angel saw the blood, that house would be spared any death. It was to be a lasting ritual in the life of Israel. Also, the Jewish people were not to eat any bread with yeast. So this ritual was first called the Feast of Unleavened Bread, also known as Passover. All Egypt got up during the night, and there was loud wailing in Egypt, for there was not a house without someone dead.

Later in history Jewish followers of Jesus prepared "to eat the Passover."[1] Unlike that first Passover in Egypt where Israel was spared death, Jesus speaks of his broken body and bleeding referring to his death for the forgiveness of sins. He also said that this Passover celebration would be his last on earth and wouldn't occur for him "until the kingdom comes." There is no indication what he meant by this. However, there does appear to be a common theme in both the Passover and Jesus' words as to people being spared death through the sacrifice of a lamb and forgiveness of sins through "the new covenant of his blood." Further reading in the New Testaments indicates that even Jesus' closest friends didn't know what he was talking about during this last Passover for all of them together.

The narrative behaviors are critical to anthropology since the Last Supper emulates current celebrations of the Eucharist. Another reference from narrative behavior anticipates future celebrations of this ritual. Speaking of a later new human community, "they devoted themselves to the apostles' teaching and to the fellowship, to the breaking of bread and to prayer."[2]

Finally as this strange ritual of eating bread and drinking wine evolves over time in the early human community, the teaching about the ritual is more conceptual. "Is not the cup of thanksgiving for which we give thanks a participation in the blood of Christ? And is not the bread that we break a participation in the body of Christ? Because there is one loaf, we who are many, are

---

1. Barker et al., *New International Version Study Bible*, 103; hereafter, NIV.

2. Ibid., 1648.

one body, for we all partake of the one loaf."[3] Anthropologically, these words are problematic. There is no way to observe how "the cup" and "breaking bread" are "participation in the blood and body of Christ." Clearly, we're at the end of ethnographic analysis and at the front door of theological meaning, which we'll address later. From this important textual background for the origin and history of eating bread and drinking wine, we turn now to this ritual's physical variables.

Physical Variables

On the Sunday where the Eucharist ritual is celebrated, the table in the front of the sanctuary has a carafe of wine, an empty chalice/cup, a plate of bread—covered with linen. There are candles on either end of the table (altar). You observe that this particular table is handmade with words in front, "Do this in remembrance of me," from the words of one of the Gospel texts. The carved words parallel the narrative behavior and later reenactment of the ritual by the community. The physical elements are quite plain and simple. No other special decor in the sanctuary indicates the celebration.

The bulletin adds a line or two indicating the ritual's placement in the service, typically after the liturgy of readings, song, prayer, and sermon.

That said, it's important to point out that ordinary bread is not found in the raw, it is part of God's good creation and is considered a sacrament.[4] Similarly, wine doesn't grow on vines. It, too, requires work. The process of going from a vineyard to corking a bottle is an observable process which can be explained scientifically. Bread as the end of a process involving grain, grinding, and baking along with wine being the final outcome of picking, mashing, and fermenting involve observable behavior, even though it doesn't occur during the worship of the human community; thus,

3. Ibid., 1788.

4. The key is the ordinariness of bread from the earth as well the ordinariness of the process. Sacraments are first ordinary and become sacred within the context of worship within the community.

its mention in the anthropological part of our analysis. Later, we'll discuss how the process of preparation enriches our theological grasp of the Eucharist.

Observed Behavior

As you sit through many celebrations of eating bread and drinking wine, you note the behavior of the pastor(s) is rather consistent involving the bread and wine. The pastor introduces the ritual with the words of institution/consecration, motions his hands as a sign of the cross over both the bread and wine, prays, and reads again. From time to time the congregation recites sayings repeated during each celebration. Key phrases used are "This is my body" when he speaks over the bread and "This is my blood" over the cup. The bread is broken into pieces on a plate symbolized when the pastor takes a large circular wafer and breaks it in half. He pours wine into the cup. At this point the pastor may serve those persons who will offer the bread and wine to the people.

Once all the words are spoken, he gives the plates of bread and cups of wine to servers who stand across the front of the sanctuary. The congregation is invited to leave their pews in single file and come one by one to the servers to receive the bread and wine. Some come with their hands cupped to receive the bread in their hands; others come up and the server puts the bread into their mouths with the words "The body of Christ broken for you" or simply "The body of Christ." Similarly, people are handed the chalice to drink the wine with the words "This is the blood of Christ shed for you" or simply "The blood of Christ." You observe that people either before or after eating and drinking spend time with heads bowed and eyes closed. Also during this time, an organ or piano plays background songs which some people sing while seated or on their way up front. Having received the elements, individuals return to their seats.

In other services you've observed the distribution of the bread and wine in special plates and trays served to people in their pews. Both the bread and wine are taken individually as the plate and tray are passed through the pew, although in some celebrations the pastor asks the church to wait until all have been served. In the last act of the ritual the pastors offer each other both the bread and wine. The pastor covers the remaining bread and wine with linens and closes the ritual with a final prayer.

Frequency of Ritual

The eating and drinking ritual is not governed by the church calendar. Its frequency seems to be arbitrary. In your time with this people group, you've seen it practiced most often on the first Sunday of the month; for no apparent reason. That is, you've never heard the pastor quote the Bible which mandates when to celebrate Communion. From church history, the ritual may have been practiced on a daily basis in the beginning enthusiasm of the early church. Over time, it may have settled into established patterns which include a once-per-month observance, in some cases every Sunday or on special occasions during the week prior to Easter called Holy Week which would include Maundy Thursday and Good Friday.

This ritual is bound to the symbol called the cross. So the events of the death of Jesus of Nazareth are recalled in Maundy Thursday, a holy day tied to the command to love one another. *Maundy* is derived from the Latin word for command.[5] It's not uncommon for the church to eat bread and drink wine during this service, which is also celebrated with a less frequent ritual—footwashing from the narrative behavior of a biblical text. The Good Friday service may also include eating and drinking Communion, recalling the day Jesus of Nazareth died on a cross. On one occasion you observed that during Holy Week the people group celebrated the Jewish Passover meal, often called the Seder Meal, complete with symbols directly tied to Israel's freedom from Egypt.

At this point in our analysis we're ready to observe different integrated patterns of knowledge, belief, and behavior which address how the ritual of Eucharist is vitally related to its accompanying symbol, the cross.

5. *Merriam-Webster*, s.v. "maundy."

Integrated Patterns of Knowledge, Belief, and Behavior for Eating Bread and Drinking Wine

The knowledge we have of the Eucharist ritual begins in the sacred texts of the Jewish people called the Torah, the biographies of Jesus called Gospels, a history of the community recorded and letters recorded in what's called a New Testament. Here we read of faith and belief, for example, in protection from death by putting blood on your front door. It took faith to do this, trusting that Moses knew what he was talking about. The knowledge of the ritual is more direct when Jesus of Nazareth's words are involved; for these very words are quoted in the ritual. The narrative behavior of Jesus and his followers is practiced in some form to this day. This ritual is not borrowed from local religion or culture. The eating of bread in response to "This is my body," and drinking wine in response to "This is my blood," is unheard of in any other religion at the time. In fact, the Romans accused the early church communities of cannibalism.

Beliefs about the Eucharist evolve over time. Disciple John writes his biography of Jesus late in the first century and speaks conceptually about Jesus as the bread of life. Here is an initial link to a theological concept which we address later. John also writes of the Last Supper as eating the flesh and drinking blood. Implicit here is a linkage between bread and body; wine and blood. So we find an integrated pattern of knowledge in text with belief. The people heard a text proclaimed and followed the behavior it stated. In the Eucharist, they heard about the behavior of Jesus at the Passover and began to practice it among themselves. They speak of gaining new life as a result of eating bread and drinking wine. Their belief in the invisible, non-observable life became a basis for faith and motivation to keep practicing the ritual. More on this when we get into theological interpretation.

Knowledge of the history and narrative behavior forms certain beliefs by the community about the ritual. They believed that doing the ritual offered them a way to keep remembering who Jesus was and his role in their lives. What was it about this ritual which was more than a memorial, but something about Jesus' role in their lives? All we know at this point is that something called eternal life is gained by the follower who consumes the bread and wine. There is no observable way to validate this claim using ethnographic methods.

To set the stage for part 2's theological analysis, the observed behavior of the gathered people group in worship as a human community doesn't end with the formal celebration, but anticipates behavior as the group scatters into the world. The behaviors observed in the service are to be reproduced in a diversity of behaviors of the scattered church in mundane pursuits. So we have a progression of integrated patterns involving knowledge, belief, and behavior. That is, all the knowledge from texts, beliefs, and practices in the ritual are not an end in itself. Rather, all that occurs in the gathered community's liturgy of the Eucharist has its parallel behavior as the scattered group walks out of the building each Sunday. In sum, we have a repeated pattern integrating knowledge, belief, gathered behavior, and scattered behavior.

This summarizes our analysis of the ritual eating bread and drinking wine called the Eucharist. We now turn our attention to its central symbol—a cross.

The Ethnography of the Cross

Origin and History

There is no biblical text indicating that the cross was ever used symbolically during the Eucharist in the first century. Symbolic use came centuries later. But the cross as a tool of execution by several cultures predates Jesus of Nazareth by several centuries.

The origin of the cross goes back to the eighth century BC with the Persians. It is first introduced into Rome in the third century BC by the Phoenicians. Death for serious crimes for the upper classes in Rome occurred privately with poison. Public death for crimes committed by members of the lower class or slaves required public execution on a cross. Death on a cross was considered the most humiliating and scandalous form of execution.[6] The cruel death by crucifixion was typically caused by cardiac arrest, breathing loss from disorders related to the diaphragm or asphyxiation caused by smoke from fires purposely set at the foot of the cross. There are varying notions of the positioning of the body which include nailing hands/wrist to the cross beam and one large nail through one foot over the other at the lower part of the vertical beam. Others images include nailing the feet separately onto the sides of the vertical beam.

Whatever the method, it is clear that the Romans intended to make the crucified the most despicable of all criminals. Death on a Roman cross implied shame; the criminal was not only bad, he was base. Crucifixion was done in busy public settings. The Romans had more than retribution in mind; they were also expressing disgust and utter contempt.

Some Romans considered crucifixion uncivilized, even for the heinous crimes of treason, forgery, or assassination. A person might survive for two days. Bodies were usually left on the cross after death for vultures or animals. There was no burial; bodies were discarded into the trash. This raises unique differences between common Roman practice and Jesus' crucifixion. The Roman crime for which Jesus was murdered was rebellion against the state; Jewish reasons included blasphemy. Jews had no power to crucify no matter what the reason under Roman occupation. Two exceptions occurred for Jesus that no other criminal experienced on a cross. First, he was given a drink to anesthetize his pain; second, his body was removed by two disciples and buried in a tomb.

It was not until after the second century AD that the fledgling community of Jewish Jesus followers made any public use of the cross as a sign or symbol. Tertullian records that in the second century "Christians crossed themselves on their foreheads."[7] The legalization of Christianity in the Roman Empire by Constantine offered new freedoms for public symbolism of the cross. Beginning in the fourth century, the crucifixion was one of the central

---

6. Hengel, *Crucifixion in the Ancient World*, 56.

7. Robert and Donaldson, *Ante-Nicene Fathers*, 31.

images in the history of Christian art. However, the transition from private to public use was often represented by disguising the cross as an anchor. Along with disguised crosses, a myriad of shapes, sizes, and positions of the cross were also employed over the centuries. Culturally, a unique feature within the Roman Empire's was a use of the cross as a sign of military victory.

There is a large discussion surrounding the empty cross compared to a cross occupied by Jesus' dying body, called a crucifix, which is a topic beyond the scope of this chapter. As an ethnographer, we observe that different communities employ one or the other. Typically, the cross on the steeple is empty. In some churches, a crucifix is on the front wall; in others, an empty cross. When the pastor wears the cross around her neck, the cross may be either; the same would occur for people wearing the cross as jewelry. "Prior to the fifth century AD, the cross was empty after which a crucifix appeared in both art and sculpture."[8] There's reason to believe that the crucifix communicated the early beliefs to the illiterate. The cross, along with other symbols, appeared as sculpture in cathedral doorways, stained glass windows, and plaques on sanctuary walls, called stations of the cross.

Given this brief account of the origin and history of the cross as the iconic symbol for the early community, we turn our attention to how the cross permeates the worship of the community.

Observed Behavior in Community Today

No specific ritual aligns with the cross. The word *cross* isn't explicit in most Eucharist celebrations, only implied. The crucifixion of Jesus of Nazareth is at the core of the community's belief. They refer to it frequently. While there is no one precise ritual/service which observes the cross, the church calendar includes a period of forty days prior to Easter called Lent. This is a time of preparation for remembering the cross, symbolizing the crucifixion of Jesus. Lent includes Maundy Thursday and Good Friday services.

8. Apostolos-Cappadona, *Dictionary of Christian Art*, 94.

During the Maundy Thursday service, the humility of the Jesus' submission to the cross is reenacted in a foot-washing observance corresponding to Jesus' washing of his followers' feet. It might include the Eucharist. The Good Friday service's focus is clearly the cross, with readings, music, and drama, and possibly communion. Finally, some traditions observe Holy Saturday in a service called the Easter Vigil, which includes an overview of significant biblical texts designed to provide a transition from the cross to the empty tomb. This service includes a celebration of the Eucharist.

Of course, the cross permeates the Eucharist: the cross is present on the altar, the pastor makes its sign over the elements, people coming up may make its sign as they receive, as liturgists walk across the platform they may pause and turn toward the cross, as people enter the sanctuary they may bow or genuflect before the cross as they take their seat. In some churches, as the cross enters the sanctuary in procession, people may make its sign as it passes their pew. During the service, either during the Eucharist or other, there are places where making the sign of the cross is left to the individual.

There appears to be no loss of reverence toward the cross, simply because no precise ritual for it exists. In fact, we see that the cross permeates the lyrics of hymns, the words read from Scripture, the sermon, and even in the architecture of the floor plan of the sanctuary, where the main center aisle may be thought of as the vertical beam of the cross, with the horizontal beam symbolized by aisle space across the front. Along with the observed behavior within the community, the narrative behavior related to the cross from the text is significant. We turn our attention now to how textual statements and narrative behavior may relate to beliefs held about the cross.

Integrated Patterns of Knowledge, Belief, and Behavior for the Cross

In the last section we observed community behavior related to the cross. We saw that while no specific ritual focuses on the cross explicitly, it permeates the speaking, hearing, reading, singing, and preaching in the worship service. In this part of our anthropological review of the cross, we notice an apparent connection between the Jewish history of capital punishment and Roman crucifixion. We begin with an analysis of a text from Jewish history recorded in the Torah, which says: "If a man guilty of a capital offense is put to death and his body is hung on a tree, you must not leave his body on the tree overnight. Be sure to bury him that same day, because anyone who is hung on a tree is under God's curse. You must not desecrate the land the Lord your God is giving you as an inheritance." We discuss the relationship of Jewish capital punishment to Roman crucifixion because the Jewish context doesn't mention a cross, but a tree.

What did this text mean for an Israelite living about fifteen centuries before Jesus of Nazareth? We attempt to answer this question from the Torah.

The usage of "a tree" in the Torah is textually linked with "the cross and tree" in the New Testament. "And if a man has committed a crime punishable by death and he is put to death, and you hang him on a tree, his body shall not remain all night on the tree, but you shall bury him the same day, for a hanged man is cursed by God."[9]

Key to a correct interpretation of this Jewish practice was a belief that crimes of treason, forgery, and murder required not only punishment at the human level, but also divine condemnation. Public stoning accomplished the murder of the criminal but dealt only with the human aspect of the law. The divine curse required hanging the body on a tree. It was a two-part punishment. After being stoned to death, the person's body was hung on a tree to show that the individual was under God's curse. The criminal not only broke a law of the land, but was forsaken and cursed by Yahweh. The gruesome display of a public hanging was seen as a deterrent to future crimes. According to Jewish law, the body was not cursed of God because it was hanging on a tree; it was hanging on a tree because it was cursed of God. The public nature of observably exposed wounds, shame, and guilt before others would not be a sufficient explanation of this punishment. It required

9. Craigie, *Book of Deuteronomy*, 285.

Yahweh's curse for breaking his covenant regarding the sacredness of the land.

There would have been little to keep a first-century Jew from going along with Roman crucifixion. The notion that the Messiah would be crucified on a Roman cross brought back texts from the Torah related to God's curse upon one hanging on a tree as punishment for the worst crimes within the Jewish community. Specifically, crucifixion as hanging on a tree is requested by a high priest for Jesus' sin of blasphemy, claiming to be Messiah.

Tree is used not only in the Jewish sacred texts, but also in the later historical documents of the human community. Jesus follower Peter's first sermon states, "This man was handed over to you; and you, with the help of wicked men, put him to death by nailing him to the cross."[10] But then before the highest Jewish court, referring to Jesus, Peter stated: "whom you had killed by hanging him on a tree." Obviously, Peter knows his Jewish audience and enhances the severity of this punishment. Also, as a Jewish convert to the new community, Paul makes similar use of *tree* in a letter, quoting the Torah: "Cursed is everyone who is hung on a tree."

There is a linkage between Jesus's actual taking up of his cross going to Golgotha and an admonition to his followers to take up their cross, as well. Jesus never referred to his death with any reference to a tree and rarely explicitly mentioned a cross as the means of his death. The interpretation of the cross as his means of world redemption is reserved for theological analysis. The most we have in any Gospel accounts of the celebration of the Last Supper and the first celebration of eating bread and drinking wine is Jesus' words referring to his body and blood being given for others.

Conclusion

So far in part 1, we've offered a brief ethnographic analysis of two rituals: the lighting of the Advent candle and the Eucharist. The manger is the symbol for the birth of Jesus of Nazareth, celebrated

10. *NIV*, 1647.

during Advent, culminating in Christmas. In this chapter we considered three symbols: bread, wine, and a cross. Bread and wine are used to remember the suffering and death of Jesus on a cross. No linkage of the first-century Last Supper with the cross occurs during Jesus' life and ministry. Biblical texts after the Gospels documenting the early history of the new community link Jesus' words during the Last Supper with his suffering and death on the cross. Teaching about the Last Supper, the cross, and the meaning of both occurs primarily in letters written by a significant Jewish Jesus follower named Paul.

We now complete the anthropology portion of the book with a brief ethnographic study of the Easter service, whose symbol is a tomb; specifically, an empty tomb.

Chapter 4

A Tomb

IN THE LAST CHAPTER we continued our study of a human community at worship celebrating the Eucharist ritual involving bread and wine symbolized by a cross. We noted a period of the church calendar called Lent, a preparation for meditation on the cross. In this chapter we'll get into the ritual of an Easter Sunday worship service whose symbol is a tomb—an empty tomb. Given that there is little ritual and minimal visibility of the empty tomb, our review of the important category *Integrated Pattern of Knowledge, Belief, and Behavior* will combine both the Easter Sunday service and the tomb. Since this is the last chapter in part 1: Anthropology, we'll conclude this chapter with a brief summary of our ethnographic analysis of a manger, bread, wine, and cross, and an empty tomb.

An Ethnography of the Easter Sunday Worship Service

Origin and History

The Easter Sunday worship service is a one-day event designed to celebrate the coming back to life of Jesus of Nazareth from the dead. The word *Easter* is found nowhere in the biblical text. It is possibly derived from the name of an ancient goddess Eostre from

Germanic paganism.[1] Its origin and history from the biblical text marks its timing as "when the Sabbath was over on the first day of the week."[2] The resurrection of Jesus of Nazareth was initially celebrated by Jewish converts into a new human community which worshipped daily in the temple. Perhaps the earliest primary source referring to Easter is a mid-second-century homily attributed to Melito of Sardis. Without going into the laborious detail, the date for Easter has been controversial, involving several different calendars. Along with its other notable accomplishments, the 325 BC Council of Nicea "decreed there must be one unanimous concord on the celebration of God's holy and supremely excellent day."[3] In effect this meant that Jewish calculations for Passover no longer determined the date for Christian celebration of Easter.

The sunrise service is a more recent addition to the historic Easter celebration. Primarily a Protestant phenomenon, it is designed to replace the Easter Vigil from more liturgical churches. Typically, it takes place outdoors. "The first Easter Sunrise Service took place in 1732 in the Moravian congregation in Saxony, Germany. After an all-night prayer meeting, the Single Brethren went to the town graveyard to sing hymns of praise to the Risen Savior. The next year, the entire congregation joined in the service."[4]

Physical Variables for Easter Services

The Easter Sunday service is a one-day celebration, possibly preceded by the sunrise service earlier in the day. In either case, changes to the decor are minimal. With the addition of fragrant lilies, white as the color all around, the sanctuary is the same as always. If a cross is present, a white shroud may be draped on its horizontal beam. There may be more flowers than usual. Unlike Advent or Eucharist, there is no symbolic portrayal specifically

---

1. *Barnhart Concise Dictionary of Etymology*, s.v. "Easter."
2. *New International Version*, 1530
3. Epiphanius, *Adversus Haereses*, 331.
4. Peucker, "Easter Morning Sunrise Service," 4.

related to the empty tomb. That is, there is no "tomb scene" with the characters from the narrative investigating a tomb with its stone rolled away. There are no figurines of women with spices; no angels, no Roman guards, and no come-to-life Jesus. There is no display of an empty tomb anywhere in the sanctuary. No one is wearing an "empty tomb" necklace. In terms of what you *don't* observe, you may be surprised that so significant a celebration about someone going from death to life is so minimally represented in sanctuary decor. A more formal dress of the congregation is the most obvious change in the physical variables surrounding Easter in the community.

Observed Behavior

The liturgy for the early sunrise or later Easter service is like always: singing, standing, readings, prayers, a choir, solos, and a sermon. What distinguishes this service is not the decor or special rituals, but the lyrics of the hymns and songs, the content of the readings, and the substance of the sermon. All point to Jesus of Nazareth being alive. People seem more excited about the worship. You hear the phrase "He is risen!" spoken by the pastor, to which the people respond, "He is risen indeed!" This may occur spontaneously several times during the service. You note that there are Easter hymns and songs sung *only* on Easter Sunday. It might even be awkward for the people to sing, for example, *Christ the Lord Is Risen Today*, during the summer. You make special note of this; because it begs the question, "Why are hymns about so special an event in the life of the people group sung only once during the year?" You also notice that there is a short list of standard Easter texts read during the service. The texts are typically from one of the four Gospels telling the story of women discovering an empty tomb, a women named Mary Magdalene actually talking with Jesus of Nazareth, or many appearances of a living Jesus. The sermon may use one of the Gospel texts and add something from letters of the Apostle Paul, who explains how Jesus' rising from the dead offers new life for the believer.

Eastertide is the name given to that period of several Sundays following Easter Sunday during which time the sermon focuses on post-death appearances of Jesus to his followers. At most, the celebration of the resurrection of Jesus involves six Sundays, with many traditions confining it to only the one-day Sunday celebration. There is no Holy Week where the immediate events of Jesus' appearances are celebrated as in Lent: Ash Wednesday, Maundy Thursday, Good Friday, and Holy Saturday. For example, there is no Easter Sunday Night Vigil to commemorate Jesus' first post-death appearance to his fearful followers. You note that Jesus' coming back to life receives so minimal attention as ritual and symbol. We'll explain this in part 2.

An Ethnography of the Tomb

Origin and History

Prior to our focus on the empty tomb itself, we set the stage by discussing the background of tombs, Jewish burial rites, and the burial of Jesus' body. No one expected Jesus' tomb to be empty on that first Easter Sunday. The concern was that a Jewish person be buried according to strict Jewish observance followed by the women whose only desire was to add fragrance to Jesus' decomposing body. Their purpose was strictly cultural in the care for Jesus' body. There was no anticipated religious or spiritual celebration for that first Easter Sunday.

As stated earlier about Roman crucifixion, burial of the body was of no concern to those who crucified criminals. Bodies were thrown into the trash, if removed from the cross at all. In the Mediterranean world of late antiquity proper burial of the dead was regarded as sacred duty, especially so in the culture and religion of the Jewish people. The burial of the body of a Jewish person involved a very careful ritual. "We must not leave a corpse unburied."[5] The origin of the Jewish burial ritual began with Abraham's burial of his wife Sarah. In this first recorded Jewish burial, the concept

5. Josephus, "Against Apion."

of *kevod ha-met*, "honoring the dead" involved a hasty burial. An unburied corpse was considered to be naked and humiliated. A proper burial in Jewish thinking was second only in importance to saving a human life.[6] Jesus' burial in a cave continued a tradition going back to Abraham through the Babylonian period and into Roman Palestine as a popular final resting place for the dead.[7]

Narrative Behavior

The Gospel biographies record that Jesus was buried by two men: Joseph of Arimathea and Nicodemus.[8] Joseph was a wealthy member of the highest Jewish ruling body who secretly followed Jesus and wanted to see that he got the best possible Jewish burial in an unused garden tomb that he owned. The precedent for burying a king in a new garden tomb goes back to the burial of kings of Judah in Jewish history. Joseph treats Jesus' body as royalty as does Nicodemus with a huge amount of spices. Nicodemus, a Pharisee, is also a secret follower who waited for the darkness of night to interview Jesus about being "born again."

The secret relationship of Joseph and Nicodemus with Jesus goes public only after his death. It was courageous to ask Pilate for the body and may have happened only because Pilate declared Jesus innocent three times. Ironically, they go public when they can only lose with Jesus' movement coming to an end with his death. There is no textual basis to believe that either Joseph of Arimathea or Nicodemus thought that Jesus would return from the dead. Their only concern was that he receive good Jewish care for the dead; even though they had no time to wash the body. Also, by handling the body they have made themselves ritually unclean and are thus disqualified from participating in the Passover. Both men cared for Jesus' body at great risk to themselves.

6. Menachemson, "Brief History of Jewish Burial," 176.
7. Ibid.
8. John 19:38–39.

The care for Jesus' body also involved several faithful women. The women who had come with Jesus from Galilee followed Joseph and saw the tomb and how his body was laid in it.[9] Along with the seventy-five pounds of spices from Nicodemus, the women waited until after the Sabbath to prepare more perfumes and spices. We note that the role of the women in Jesus' life, death, and burial was consistently public. It is these same women who were the first to discover the empty tomb. We note that the community relies on the recorded texts which attest to the behavior of key people who believe in Jesus' resurrection, in this case Mary of Magdala, Mary the mother of James, and Salome. Most scholars today agree that the tomb of Jesus was found empty. An often-neglected portion of the narrative behavior of those persons directly related to Jesus' burial involves the Jewish admission of an empty tomb. It involved a cover-up when Roman guards went to the Jewish chief priests to say that Jesus' body was missing. The lie would be that the disciples stole Jesus' body from the tomb while the guards were sleeping. That is, the chief priests paid off the guards for admitting they were derelict in their duty, a military crime punishable by death. Jewish religious leaders acknowledged an empty tomb, requiring a lie followed by a cover-up.[10] Only a few Jewish women responded to an empty tomb with belief followed by spreading the word of an alive Jesus of Nazareth.

The Narrative Post-Death Appearances of Jesus of Nazareth

In this section we consider five stories from Jesus' biographies which indicate the narrative behavior of those persons who encountered a post-death Jesus of Nazareth. First, Mary Magdalene at the tomb, followed by two disciples walking to Emmaus, the Sunday night appearance to eleven followers, the next week's encounter with Thomas, and Jesus cooking breakfast for the disciples,

9. Luke 24:1–11.
10. Craig, "Guard at the Tomb," 273–81.

involving Peter's reinstatement. We'll point out the uniqueness of each encounter, observing the behavior of both Jesus and those present. At the outset, we note that among the accounts of Jesus' life, each is selective in terms of the number and level of detail of the appearances they record. Anthropologically, these texts at this point are not proof statements of any theology. Rather, they document the claims of the sacred literature of our people group, a community of human beings worshiping their deity.

First, there is Jesus' encounter with Mary Magdalene, who remained at the cross while Jesus died and stayed behind at the empty tomb after others left. She was wailing in grief not only over Jesus' death but also the loss of his body. Her question was this: "Where is Jesus' body?" There is no reason to believe that Mary expected anything other than a tomb occupied by Jesus' body. She only wanted to grieve. She has a brief conversation with two angels who she sees sitting where the body had been. For our purposes as ethnographers, we note that what she saw suggests that Mary was conscious, not hallucinating or dreaming; essentially, she saw the angels like she would see anything. Also, she heard these spirits speaking in a language she could understand. The angels see that she was crying, which suggests they grasp human emotion to ask the question: "Why are you crying?" We note that the angels recorded in this narrative provide no answers, they merely listen to Mary. For reasons the text doesn't state, Mary turns around while talking with the angels and sees Jesus without realizing that it was he. No explanation is offered, but we may assume she's at very least bewildered at Jesus' death and now anxious over the loss of his body. While looking at but not recognizing who he is, Mary hears Jesus ask: "Who is it you are looking for?" She doesn't recognize Jesus' voice, but believes it to be that of the gardener who she assumes has relocated Jesus' body and requests that he tell her where it is so she can carry him away. That is, just as Jesus' body was removed from the cross and buried by Joseph of Arimathea, Mary is willing to carry Jesus' body from wherever it is back to the tomb, where it belongs. She's maintaining Jewish respect for the dead.

Everything changes when Mary Magdalene hears someone speak her name. We note Mary knows it is Jesus by the sound of her name, not by sight. Then she cries out for joy, addressing Jesus as her rabbi. She wants to embrace him but is told not to do so. As her rabbi, Jesus continues teaching her by making a significant statement. "I am returning to my Father and your Father, to my God and your God." That Yahweh is one's personal Father and personal God is a huge departure from Judaism's typical reverential language for God, whose name must not be spoken. Earlier in his life, Rabbi Jesus taught the disciples how to pray, saying, "*Our* Father." Jesus' communal vocabulary and intimate language represents a radical shift in Judaism. It's also a great shift in Mary's relationship with Jesus of Nazareth, who in this first post-death encounter has gone from "gardener" to rabbi to telling the disciples that she had seen the Lord.

Second, later that day two distraught disciples are walking back to their home in Emmaus. One of them is Cleopas. The other is unnamed. They are recalling everything that happened. Like all other appearances, Jesus *suddenly* shows up and walks beside them. They don't recognize him. No explanation regarding what hinders their ability to identify Jesus is given. Jesus wants to know what they are talking about. Cleopas can't believe that anyone, even a visitor, would be ignorant of the exciting news about Jesus' dying and coming back to life. Jesus' response has to be one of the most ironic examples of humor in any literature—sacred or otherwise. To their discussion of the "exciting things" which have just occurred in Jerusalem, Jesus says, "What things?" Picture the center of all the attention asking such a question. They both rehearse the weekend's events, though they get it wrong about the angels, which they claim was merely a vision. Jesus then rebukes their ignorance and unbelief related to their Jewish Torah, Writings, and Prophecy, which forecasts someone who would suffer these things and enter his glory. Jesus then instructs these Jewish followers in what was said in all the Scriptures concerning himself.

The conversation goes from instruction to an invitation that Jesus spend the evening with them given the lateness of the hour. Jesus accepts their hospitality and joins them for supper. It is while eating a meal together that they recognize Jesus; not by hearing his voice or touching him, but by something he does. Jesus took bread, gave thanks, broke it, and began to give it to them. Then their eyes were opened and they recognized him. Just like that, Jesus vanishes! At that point yet another type of recognition comes to mind. They recall how their hearts were burning while he talked and opened the Scriptures. Here we have an emotional feeling prompted by listening to Jesus as he teaches them about himself from their sacred literature. As they share their story with the disciples, they focus on Jesus' breaking of the bread.

Third, another post-death appearance of Jesus occurs that night to several of his disciples cowering in fear and guilt behind a locked door. They fear that the religious authorities may be after them, as well. Possibly they feel guilty for sleeping in Gethsemane, Judas' betrayal, Peter's denial, and leaving the cross. They're bracing for a rebuke from Jesus, who crosses them up and offers a standard, but surprising Jewish greeting, "Peace be with you"; that is, a modern-day Shalom. Jesus shows them his wounded hands and feet. This confirms that the mysterious human being who walked through a locked door is Jesus of Nazareth. Unlike Mary Magdalene, the disciples recognize Jesus by seeing him. For them, seeing is believing. They're joyfully surprised. While Jesus understands their joy, his concern shifts quickly to mission. These converted-from-fear-to-joy followers will spread the word just as Jesus had prayed. Then Jesus does something surprising. He breathes a holy spirit on them and assigns them a task: forgiving the sins of others. It's difficult to envision Jesus breathing a holy spirit. Even an eyewitness would have difficulty recording this as behavioral data. This event anticipates a larger dispensing of a Holy Spirit for the entire community for later discussion.

Parenthetically, one notable disciple, Thomas, was missing on this first appearance of Jesus to his followers. Just after their encounter with Jesus, the disciples told Thomas that Mary Magdalene had seen the Lord! That is, by observing Jesus' wounds God became more than a distant Yahweh; he became more personal. It would be the wounds that would identify this come-back-to-life Jesus as the same one who was killed on the cross. But Thomas not only wants to see the wounds, but feel them. In what many would consider distasteful, not to mention unsanitary, Thomas actually wants to put his finger in the puncture wounds on Jesus' hands and insert his hand in the larger open wound on Jesus' side. He gets his chance to do this in Jesus' next appearance.

Fourth, one week after Jesus left the tomb, this time all the disciples including Thomas are gathered behind the same locked door. Jesus once more proclaims, "Peace be with you!" With no textual reference that Jesus knew about Thomas' doubt, he takes the initiative and asks Thomas to do precisely what he required to identify Jesus. Thomas' response is the same as Mary's and the disciples': "My Lord and my God!" His relationship to God is changed in this encounter with a crucified-but-alive Jesus of Nazareth. Jesus credits Thomas' shift from doubt to belief; but credits more those who would later believe without seeing. So far within one active week, we observe four separate post-death appearances of Jesus involving differing situations, yet all related to a transition from grief, fear, bewilderment, and doubt to belief. Jesus has made appearances to his closest followers to reassure them of who he was and that his tomb was empty, not because his body had been stolen by his disciples, but because he had come back to life. But even all these observations do not settle all doubts completely.

A fifth recorded appearance occurs on the shores of the Sea of Galilee, which we consider in two parts. One has to do with fish, the other with reinstating Peter. We're not a given a specific time as in other post-death appearances. It may have occurred sometime after Jesus' conversation with Thomas. A group of the disciples decides to go fishing throughout the night. Jesus showed up early in the morning, but the disciples did not recognize that it was Jesus. After significant encounters with Jesus, they still have doubts about Jesus' identity. Like Mary Magdalene, an apparent beginning of recognition occurs by hearing Jesus' voice. They've gotten nothing all night and Jesus suggests they try the other side of the boat. They were unable to haul in the net, because there were so many fish. Both John and Peter verbalize their assurance that this is Jesus with "It's the Lord!" Here we have Jesus cooking breakfast for them on the shore. Jesus made a fire, cooked fish, and produced bread with the anticipation of eating with his followers. Jesus took the bread and the fish and distributed it to them. Recall the two traveling to Emmaus who recognized Jesus when he took bread and how Jesus used eating fish to identify himself earlier. You note how Jesus uses an ordinary physical function of eating to show his uniquely risen body is human.

A next phase of this encounter involves a special conversation with Peter. Jesus has three related questions for Peter with three similar recommendations for how Peter should change his lifestyle. Three times Jesus asks Peter whether he loves him. Peter confirms his love each time. Jesus asks Peter three times to show his love by doing something. A progression of commands follows from Jesus to Peter: "Feed my lambs, take care of my sheep, and follow me!" Obviously, Jesus' recommendations are metaphorical, for Peter never becomes a shepherd. Other biblical texts indicate that Peter took Jesus' words seriously and radically changed his relationship with a resurrected Jesus of Nazareth.

In sum, we've briefly discussed the narrative behaviors of Jesus and his followers in a sequence of events after his death. At stake in the five events is an answer to the question, Is this Jesus of Nazareth? In each case the answer is yes, where initial feelings of fear, anxiety, and doubt are transformed to belief in a resurrected Jesus of Nazareth. We now conclude our ethnographic look into the Easter Sunday ritual and its symbol of the empty tomb by discussing a final appearance of Jesus which is really a disappearance. At this point we have enough data to integrate patterns of knowledge, belief, and behavior.

Integrated Patterns of Knowledge, Belief, and Behavior for the Easter Sunday Service and Tomb

The final post-death appearance of Jesus of Nazareth to his disciples occurs in an event where he suddenly disappears. In this event Jesus lifts off the ground before their very eyes. Just before this gravity-defying event, Jesus has given instructions for mission to go, to urge others to believe and to become followers with the promise that Jesus would never leave them. The next major recorded event was that the disciples worshipped joyfully and praised God continually at the temple.

The text records how confused the disciples were about Jesus' words regarding the kingdom, going back to the first words which launched his ministry.[11] Throughout Jesus' ministry, even the closest followers looked at Jesus as a political reformer who would reinstate the monarchy of Israel from the past. Their immediate concern was to get out from under Roman occupation. As Jews, they knew full well their history with Egyptian slavery, Assyrian deportation and Babylonian captivity. Given this context, their statement, "Lord, are you at this time going to restore the kingdom to Israel?" Jesus' doesn't answer the question, but speaks of their future mission as his witnesses. Unique to this historical account is a promise that Jesus will return to earth in a reversal of how the disciples observed him ascend into the firmament.

The integration of knowledge, belief, and behavior occurs in these texts as a summary of Jesus' entire life and ministry on earth. The textual narrative behavior throughout the biographies speaking of Jesus' contact with a diversity of people includes an integration which starts with new knowledge that he brings. That knowledge challenges beliefs which are a radical departure from current religion of the day. Radical changes in belief usher followers into a new lifestyle of behavior. This pattern dominates the knowledge-belief-behavior category found throughout the Gospels. From the very beginning, Jesus speaks about a kingdom, always misunderstood by his closest followers, right up to the end where they are now empowered by a holy spirit to fulfill an ongoing mission. The Jewish disciples want political and national freedom; Jesus speaks of their role in building up *his* kingdom. Jesus never defines the characteristics of his kingdom, though his stories give hints as to its characteristics.

11. *NIV*, 1494. "The kingdom of God is near. Repent and believe the good news." This is a key statement interpreted theologically in part 2.

Throughout the post-death accounts culminating in this final event, we observe narrative behavior in all five situations involving Mary Magdalene, the disciples three times, and Thomas based upon the knowledge Jesus forecasts of his suffering and death resulting in belief. The Easter Sunday service celebrates such knowledge. Knowledge of his coming back to life reassures belief when the community says: "He is risen. He is risen indeed!" The sacred narratives of Jesus' life recording the post-death appearances offer knowledge which ends in belief for many. This pattern has repeated itself for over two thousand years. Such belief motivates the ritual of Easter Sunday's celebration. The community is motivated in reading, song, and proclamation not only to believe, but also to behave like the first believers. That is, parishioners often "see themselves in the text." They may speak of desiring the faith of Mary Magdalene. They may see their doubt transformed by a Thomas who believes when he actually touches Jesus' unique resurrected body. Others may see their denial repaired by love for the community just as caring for others restored Peter.

Conclusion

In sum, a pattern culminating in Jesus' leaving after several appearances models all previous integrations of knowledge, belief, and behavior discussed in terms of a manger on the part of Mary, the mother of Jesus, shepherds or Persian astrologers. Each in their way acted on knowledge prompted by a transformation of initial bewilderment and doubt to joy. We observed the cross within the Eucharist ritual, where in a similar way parishioners eat bread and drink wine just as in that first historic transition from Passover to the Lord's Supper. The words used then are the same words now: "This is my body; this is my blood." While the manger anticipates the death of Jesus of Nazareth, the Eucharist looks back to the cross. As we've just seen, the transformation of disbelief to belief about a risen Jesus continues to motivate today's parishioners to continue to worship in community.

This concludes part 1: Anthropology, where our focus has been to view a community called the church as an "ethnographic object." We've considered a pairing of ritual and symbol related to three major events in this human community: the pairing of lighting an Advent candle and a manger, the Eucharist with the cross, and the Easter Sunday service with an empty tomb. Part 2: Theology, follows. Its objective is to interpret the ethnographic data theologically. Throughout the first part of the book, you've read "more on this later." Part 2: Theology, is the "later" to which we now turn our attention.

Part Two

Theology

Chapter 5

The Church

In part 1: Anthropology, we viewed a human community as an ethnographic object by observing its rituals and symbols. The interpretation of those rituals and symbols occurs in part 2: Theology. Essentially, theology thinks and speaks of God. In this chapter we will discuss *worship, prayer, preaching,* and Bonhoeffer's idea of the *church.* The theology is determined from Jesus' words and others as recorded in Scripture. The intent of this book is to make theological vocabulary and language accessible for all human beings. Recall that we are attempting to follow Bonhoeffer's suggestion to speak biblical concepts into nonreligious language with a human accent. All biblical references in part 2 are from the NIV as in part 1; however, now the author's name with chapter and verse will identify a specific text.

To begin, we provide a theological view of basic terms from part 1. For example, we now name the human community from chapter 1 *theologically* as the church. The church is a human community with "Christ existing as the church."[1] The Bible is inspired by the Holy Spirit as God's voice. That is, we now say that one can hear the voice of God from its pages. That sacred text is the inspired, authoritative Word of God for faith and practice in the

---

1. Bischoff, *Secular Church*, 48.

church. The Word of God is nevertheless a book.[2] For example, we know this human community is the church because that's what the Word of God says it is. So our interpretation focuses on Jesus' view of reality. The Lord Jesus Christ is *the unique criterion for truth.*

Theologically, we now name Jesus of Nazareth as Jesus Christ, the Lord and Savior of the world, the Second Person of the Trinity, the Son of God. Jesus of Nazareth is simultaneously and mysteriously the Son of God. Parishioners will now be called Christians or Christ-followers to identify them as persons, like the first believers, whose lives have been changed by a personal encounter with the Crucified Christ, the Risen Lord of the church and the universe. Church parishioners are still human like any other human being. Just as anthropology describes *what* we observed, theology explains the *why* or the *how* behind our observations.

In chapter 1 we observed the church in worship. Worship is the essential ritual of the church in all its facets to be discussed below. We noted that for certain seasons of the church, specific mini-rituals and symbols frame and guide the worship. Regarding physical characteristics and furniture of the sanctuary, we simply mention here a theology which supports the pulpit as the preaching function, the altar for the Eucharist and the font used for baptism. Recall the stained glass windows—these images communicate the biblical stories of the faith primarily for the illiterate going back generations. For us today, they add visualization to key events in Jesus' life. Functions and rituals are discussed in more depth below when we consider the sacraments of the church.

Also, in chapter 1 we observed that the human community was predominately white middle class with a few African Americans and many children of Asian descent across several decades in age. There is no sociological or anthropological explanation for this diversity. The church is not run by some government system of ethnic, gender, or age quotas. The diversity in a church is not forced, but supported by Paul's letter to the Ephesians, where he states that Christ is our peace and has destroyed the dividing wall of hostility to create in himself one new humanity. That is,

2. Ibid., 34.

a homogeneous grouping in a church is an oxymoron. Churches are by nature diverse in every way possible where there is neither Jew nor Greek, slave nor free, male nor female. Why is the church ethnically, socioeconomically, and by gender diversified? Because the cross of Jesus Christ has dismantled all dividing walls. In chapter 1, we observed the church in worship. Why does this human community worship? What is worship and why does the church celebrate as it does? We now interpret church behaviors in worship. That is, we consider a theology of worship for the church.

A Theology of Worship

"The primary purpose of life is to glorify God and to enjoy him forever."[3] Recall that we referred to worship as liturgy, the work of the people. The work of worship occurs as celebration by the gathered church vitally linked to its liturgy as a scattered church. The church glorifies God and enjoys him when it scatters no less than when it gathers. The church is *always* worshiping. In chapter 1 we spoke of two ways to see behavior: observed and narrative. We now add a third type of behavior of the scattered church. It is the behavior of obedient action in between Sunday celebrations. It is behavior directly informed by the narrative behavior of Jesus Christ and his followers as well as motivated by the observed behavior of gathered Christians in celebration. As the authority for belief and behavior for the church, the Word of God sets the stage of both celebratory liturgy and obedient liturgy in the gathered and scattered community, respectively.

Authentic Christian worship is the church's response to the acts of God. "While worship is rooted in the human soul it does not begin with human need, but with God."[4] Narrative behavior located in the Psalms greatly informs the worship of the church. Part of the liturgy includes the singing of a doxology (literally, "a

---

3. Wiberg, *Covenant Book of Worship*, 3.
4. Ibid.

liturgical expression or word of praise to God.").[5] The 150 psalms recorded in the Bible are subdivided into five sections, each with its own conclusion ending in a doxology. The use of *doxology* in church bulletins as an item of the liturgy is not accidental, but a significant part of historic celebration in the church.

"God is the great Initiator. Before we do anything, God has already acted."[6] God acts through words. Creation occurred because God said so and named all segments of what we observe as a natural revelation of himself. God spoke and made light, sky, vegetation, sun, moon, stars, animals, and human beings called man and woman. The Holy Spirit brought into being the person of Jesus of Nazareth, Son of God, who has always been the Second Person of the Godhead (Father, Son, and Holy Spirit). That is, "in the beginning the Word was with God and the Word was God."[7] Jesus was the Word who became flesh and made his dwelling among us. The title of chapter 6 uses the word *incarnation*, which is the theological term for the process bringing the God-human, Jesus, into the world. While certain rituals are sacramental, the essential and first sacrament is Jesus Christ, the ordinary Jesus of Nazareth as a human being who is simultaneously the sacred Deity of the world. In worship the reading and hearing of the Word are coupled with the seeing of the Word in the sacraments, all of which point out that God has acted on our behalf. God initiates worship just as he created everything.

Worship is a public communal response to God who has acted in Jesus Christ. Worship as the church is not an individualistic, private event, even though private devotions certainly constitute worship. We are not simply a collection of people individually worshiping God, but the people of God united in one Spirit into one living church, which corporately offers its worship to God. Public communal worship and private individual devotions impact one another. Private time with God prepares us for communal worship; public communal worship inspires devotional solitude.

5. *Merriam-Webster*, s.v. "doxology."

6. Wiberg, *Covenant Book of Worship*, 4.

7. John 1:1.

Finally, communal worship as the gathered church is essentially celebratory. The liturgy of the gathered church is mirrored in that of the scattered church. For example, the invocation is reflected by beginning the day with prayer individually. The reading of Psalms, the Old Testament, Gospel, and the Epistle models individual reading/study of Scripture throughout the week. The offering urges serving our neighbors. The sacramental altar of the Eucharist, giving thanks to God for his sacrifice for us as sinners, models becoming a living sacrament in the world. The sermon inspires an urgency to learn and communicate the gospel to others. The pastor proclaims the Word to the gathered church; the scattered church tells the good news to others as opportunities surface within personal friendships. Finally, why does the church sing?

The church sings because it hasn't forgotten where it's been. It knows that only because of Christ's life, death, and resurrection it is not a collection of unforgiven sinners, but a community of forgiven sinners. The Christian is no longer bound to sin; that is why she sings. "The caged bird sings with a fearful trill of things unknown."[8] Maya Angelou captures the power of song when the liberty of flight for a caged bird is bound by dysfunctional wings and feet. She speaks of a free bird who may have never known what it's like to be in a cage or has forgotten what it was once like. Such a bird forgets to sing while enjoying freedom to do whatever it wants. Applying her metaphor to worship, the church is a bird who was caged but hasn't forgotten! It knows where it's been and it realizes what it now has in Christ. Forgiven sinners know why caged birds sing; for the caged bird sings longingly for liberty and freedom. Theologically, singing is a most natural behavior for the church. The church can't help but sing the gospel. While beautiful voices end up in the choir, the less beautiful voices in the congregation are invited to sing along. Church at its best has 100 percent of the community singing. Since music orders tones or sounds to produce a composition having unity and continuity, a full participation of singing represents the best theological model for worship. Having only one-half of a congregation singing makes no sense. Singing in worship is music

8. Angelou, *I Know Why the Caged Bird Sings*, 85.

because its tones and sounds symbolize a *unity* of being and purpose. Singing in worship is music because its message is *continuous.* When individual Christians are singing a hymn from Sunday on Monday morning in private devotions, they perpetuate the gospel. When a singing bird outside your bedroom window alerts the world to another day just before sunrise, it is worshiping its Creator, echoing gladness for another day.

A Theology of Prayer

Given a theology of worship, we now get into individual liturgical elements of the worship service. Prayer is one such element. As ethnographers we observed the community bowing its head in passive silence with closed eyes. What were they doing? They were praying by address God with adoration, confession, supplication or thanksgiving. When the pastor begins the service with an invocation which invites the congregation into worship, she is actually calling the Holy Spirit into the worship service. Worship leaders and pastors may lead the service, but the Holy Spirit presides over the service.

There are several liturgical forms of prayer. Responsive praying is a mutual participation of one person with the congregation addressing God. A *pastoral prayer* may be offered by the pastor representing the needs of the church to God. At times, a *prayers of the people* liturgy is one person or the congregation echoing praise and petition to the Lord. "Prayer in the biblical perspective is spontaneous, though it may take structured forms."[9] Prayers may be written out and read or unscripted emotional outbursts of praise or lament during a worship service. True prayer . . . bursts through all forms and techniques. Crying out to God in complaint, confusion, or frustration, however unpracticed, is a thoroughly biblical and legitimate way to address God. From the Psalms we have, "O Lord, the God who saves me, day and night I cry out before you; turn your ear to my cry; my soul is full of trouble; my life draws near the grave; the darkness is my closest friend."[10] Can

9. Elwell et al., *Evangelical Theological Dictionary*, 947.
10. Psalm 88:18.

you imagine the choir in your church singing Psalm 88 as a prayerful anthem? Or would it not be unusual, yet appropriate, for an individual to pray this lament during an open time of vocal prayer?

Communicating with God is both wrestling with God in the darkness and resting in the stillness. While the church is traditionally comfortable with prayers of praise and adoration, to be incarnational, it needs to practice the biblical heritage of penitence, lament, complaint, and frustration to God as a normal act of worship. This type of prayer is real, just like our issues and problems are real. Again the Psalmist prays, "Out of the depths I cry to you, O Lord; O Lord, hear my voice. Let your ears be attentive to my cry for mercy."[11] This is the lament of an admitted sinner. At the same time the pray-er acknowledges the grace and mercy available from a forgiving God. Looking seriously into such psalms moves our worship closer to reality. Often liturgy can become so formal, rigid and rote that it fails to connect with the real needs of the gathered congregation. Authentic worship includes prayers of anxiety and lament because the narrative behavior of those who wrote the Bible constantly points the church in this direction. Christian prayer is both solitary and communal. The church is encouraged to offer both individual needs as well as offer to God the needs of the church and the nation. Prayer includes being absorbed into the being of God balanced by requesting a transformation of the world for the glory of God. Our spirituality is enhanced and relationship with God strengthened as we continue to grasp who God is. At the same time, prayer is not a vehicle of detachment or withdrawal from the world. Prayer is a this-worldly activity fully engaged with what's going on in the public arena. However jaded a Christian may become over the politics in the nation, the church is commanded to pray for all those in authority that we may live peaceful and quiet lives. Prayer is about God, not us.

---

11. Psalm 130:1–2.

A Theology of Preaching

The Word of God provides the substance for all that's read, sung, prayed or proclaimed in a Christian worship service. The number of texts depends upon church liturgical tradition. At most the readings would include a Psalm, possibly as a *call to worship*, followed by an Old Testament, Gospel, and Epistle reading. The Gospel reading may provide the text for the sermon. How is *reading* the Bible different from *preaching* Scripture? Both are the Word of God, yet the task of a reader is qualitatively different from the objective for the preacher. To read a biblical text need not include explanation or application to life. A preacher passionately proclaims an idea or a course of action in public. But politicians do this, salespersons do this, and teachers proclaim ideas and courses of action in classrooms across the nation. What's unique about what a pastor does when he is preaching a biblical text? A sermon is speech whose most widespread use is within and for the church always rooted in the Word of God. Politicians give speeches which are clearly not the Word of God. Teachers convey ideas with no reference to an inspired source. The sermon is unique by virtue of its source and its public nature within the church. A private sermon is an oxymoron. A sermon without reference to Scripture is not a sermon.

Theologically, preaching is "the manifestation of the Incarnate Word from the written word through the spoken word."[12] This excellent definition combines Jesus as God-human, the Scripture, and a human being. Let's look at each of these three components.

First, the Incarnate Word is the word who became flesh from John's Gospel. No one would have known a word who became spirit, for such a Word would be invisible with no identification with human beings. At the incarnation, two of these three preaching components were present in the manger—Jesus as God and a human being. To begin, Jesus is the fulfillment of all that had been previously written about his arrival through the Law and the Prophets and a human being as a baby is present in the manger. All

---

12. Elwell, *Evangelical Dictionary of Theology*, 948.

that was missing from the manger was the spoken word, because not even baby Jesus spoke. A speaking baby would have been too supernatural humanly speaking and a violation of God's complete identification with humanity in every way, except in sin. The spoken word launched by the Incarnate Word written about for centuries takes place when Jesus begins talking. The first record of Jesus' speech occurs when this young adolescent son of a carpenter baffles the synagogue leaders with his knowledge. The first recorded proclamation of the gospel occurs when Jesus says that the time has come for the kingdom of God; repent and believe the good news! Essentially, every preached sermon since this first one must have this basic gospel at its core.

Second, Jesus' words evidence his knowledge of the Law, Writings, and Prophets. Matthew's account of the church's first sermon includes Jesus quoting the Prophets. The so-called Sermon on the Mount includes Jesus saying several times: "You have heard it said, but I tell you." It's important to point out that Jesus is not referring to the Old Testament when he says, "You have heard it said." Rather, he's talking about what the people have heard from errant interpretations of the Law from temple teachers. Jesus' preaching consistently brought the people back to the Torah and the Prophets. Just as the written Word was the basis for Jesus' preaching, so also must all proclamation which claims to be Christian.

Third, every preacher stands in Jesus' place before the church. It is God's voice which is to be heard through the preacher's voice. The preacher is the medium, the content comes from God. An appropriate prayer prior to the sermon comes from the hearers for themselves that they might hear the voice of God. The sermon is the primary liturgical element through which the congregation hears the voice of God. The ideas advanced are God's, not the pastor's. The preacher's words are from the Word of God. The Holy Spirit who inspired writers to record God's Word also inspires the proclaimer. That same Spirit distills every word so that what is heard is only from God. No sermon should end without an "Amen" at its end. Effective preaching allows calls for a response— during the service as well as into the future. After Jesus spoke

God's word, people actively responded. A paralytic rolled up his mat and walked. Others wanted to shout from the rooftops. A few came back to thank Jesus for what he had for them. Peter's first sermon paralleled Jesus' first sermon. Both elicited behavioral responses. In Jesus' case, disciples changed their vocations to follow Jesus. When Peter completed his sermon, people wondered what they should do. Peter's answer was to repent, to be baptized, and to receive the Holy Spirit. Three thousand people did!

To summarize, we've noted that Jesus as God in the flesh, the written word, and a preacher constitute the sermon which proclaims the gospel. So far, we've attempted a theological interpretation of those observed elements in the worship service, with a focus upon worship, prayer, and preaching. We finish this chapter with Dietrich Bonhoeffer's theology of the church.

Bonhoeffer's Theology of the Church

In this section we'll get into how Bonhoeffer's view of Jesus Christ impacts his idea of the church. His signature statement of the church is this: "Christ exists *as* the church."[13] At times it's the little things in life that count. In our discussion of Bonhoeffer's statement, it's the little word: *as*. That is, Bonhoeffer does not say: "Christ exists *in* the church." These small words have huge implications for ecclesiology, a theology of the church. "With *as*, there is nothing about the church which is not about Christ; using *in*, Christ is reduced to a subset of the church leaving room in the church which is non-Christ. This, of course, is impossible. For Bonhoeffer, Christ and the church are equal in both form and function.

Bonhoeffer's church is a church of the cross. Here he speaks of Jesus Christ as the vicarious representative for humanity. What's this mean? The answer is all about what Christ *becomes for us*. First, Christ becomes *sin* for us. Second, Christ becomes *an advocate* for us. Let's look at each more closely. When Christ became sin for us, he did so as our substitute. He took our place on the cross. When

---

13. Bonhoeffer, *Sanctorum Communio*, 140, my italics.

Christ became an advocate for us on our behalf, his ministry of grace continues. Christ continually pleads our case before the Father. Substitution is a one-time event; however, vicarious representation includes not only substitution, but an *ongoing* ministry of Jesus Christ as the unique meditator between God and humanity.[14]

The results of Christ's vicarious representation create one new humanity called the church. Originally, this new humanity had a direct bearing on the conflict between Jewish people and Gentiles. Recall that the original church was comprised of only Jewish converts to Jesus, which eventually evolved into a Jewish-Gentile community. This new unity fulfills that Christ destroyed the barrier, the dividing wall of hostility, to create in himself one new humanity through the cross. Parenthetically, we see such diversity represented at the manger among those persons who gathered to worship a baby-king: angels, a young mother and father, shepherds; and later Persian astrologers. The manger anticipates the cross as a location of people of all backgrounds. Liturgically, we observed how the varied colors of candles comprising the Advent wreath similarly displays a diversity around the center candle, which symbolizes Christ. The manger forecasts the cross of Jesus which creates unity among all cultures. The person and work of Jesus Christ on the cross, a Roman tool of torture and death for criminals, is crucial to Bonhoeffer's ecclesiology.

Bonhoeffer's church is a scandalous community of human beings who are reconciled and at the same time sinners. That is, his church is not religious, but Christian. It derives from the Apostle Paul's discussion of the gospel. "For the message of the cross is foolishness to those who are perishing, but to us who are being saved it is the power of God. God was pleased through foolishness to save those who believe. We preach Christ crucified, a scandal to Jews and foolishness to Gentiles."[15] Bonhoeffer's church is scandalous because Jesus hangs from a tree. It is also scandalous because God hangs from a Roman cross as the most despicable of all criminals. God is nailed to a cross, a symbol of Roman contempt and

14. 1 Timothy 2:5.
15. 1 Corinthians 1:18–23.

disgust. How can God be on this cross? The mystery of the cross and its church is captured in the answer to the above question. Here we can only say: because of God's grace. A church of such a cross must be by nature scandalous, for it contains only sinners; but *forgiven* sinners by grace through faith! A scandalous Christ exists as a scandalous church. This community of recovering sinners is the only hope for the world because Jesus Christ is the only hope for the world. That is, a scandalous church must not only be inwardly spiritual, but also outwardly incarnational.

Bonhoeffer's church is a *religion-less* church. He defines *religion* as inward piety withdrawn from the world. A religious church withdraws from God's creation and humanity; it does not love the world as God's creation nor other human beings. Bonhoeffer desires a church fully engaged in the world, challenging the most successful godless person with the claims of Jesus Christ as Lord who is the center of life. He seeks a church which answers this question: "What does it mean to be the church in a nonreligious way?"[16] His life ends before he's able to fully answer this important question. Part of his answer stems from the incarnation. Bonhoeffer's church agrees with the Apostle Paul as the new humanity available to and inclusive of all people from every tongue, tribe, ethnicity, and nation. Along with the divinity of Jesus of Nazareth, the church as the presence of Christ is the true humanity on earth. It is the mystery of Jesus of Nazareth who was at the same time the Second Person of the Holy Trinity.

The church is composed of broken human beings who are the temple of the Holy Spirit. It is the Holy Spirit who becomes the invisible common denominator among otherwise very different people who may be rich and poor, male and female, and healed from or paralyzed in woundedness. It is a community of wounded healers. The church is the wounded body of Jesus Christ just as the resurrected body of Jesus bore the puncture wounds on his hands and feet with his lacerated side touched by Thomas. Just as Jesus' living body bore his scars, the living church, the body of Jesus, bears its own wounds and the hurts of a broken world. It is a

16. Bonhoeffer, *Letters and Papers from Prison*, 32.

church that participates in the sufferings of Jesus on behalf of the world as its vicarious representative; that is, the church enters into the sin and guilt of humanity and calls people to a Savior, Jesus Christ. This church is a vicarious representative for all humanity. It replaces Christ on earth. It advocates for the marginalized and guilty before God.

In sum, Bonhoeffer's church is informed by these two statements: Christ exists as the church and Jesus Christ is the vicarious representative for all humanity. These two statements are introduced here to be followed up in more detail when we interpret the manger, bread, wine, cross, and tomb, theologically.

Conclusion

In this first chapter of part 2: Theology, we've seen how the human community is the church. We've observed that the church never loses sight of where it's been as a community of sinners and rejoices that in Christ it is a community of *forgiven* sinners. Just as we observed a human community in worship, we've analyzed theologically why the church worships Jesus Christ. We've proposed a theology of worship where a gathered community celebrates the gospel and a scattered community lives out the gospel in mundane day-to-day life. Praying is speaking to and hearing from God as a fundamental activity of the church. We defined preaching as a synthesis of proclaiming God in the flesh from the Scriptures through a sermon. Finally, we've defined the church from Bonhoeffer's two signature statements: *Christ exists as the church* and *Jesus is the vicarious representative for all humanity*. Bonhoeffer's church is a religion-less scandalous community of the cross whose Lord is the center of life for all humanity. Having presented a theology of the church, we now turn our attention to the symbols discovered from our previous ethnographic analysis, beginning with the manger as the basis for the incarnation.

Chapter 6

The Incarnation

IN THE LAST CHAPTER we interpreted an ethnographic analysis of a human community called the church. In this chapter we'll analyze the manger theologically by investigating several biblical texts and discussing Bonhoeffer's view of the incarnation. Incarnation is "the embodiment of a deity or spirit in some earthly form."[1] We identify that deity as the God of Abraham, Isaac, and Jacob, the God of the Bible. God takes the earthly form of a baby in a manger. The Apostle John refers to God as a human who made his dwelling among us. Unlike the Greek gods who come and go as adults, showing up only to solve problems, the God of Scripture came as a baby, grew up like any other Jewish boy, and remained on earth for about thirty-three years. He came to do more than solve our problems, but to be the center of our lives. Christianity is unique among world religions in that it points humanity to a God who willingly becomes weak and helpless. While other religious expressions embrace power and might, the God of the Bible descended from heaven to earth, from exaltation to humiliation and from a throne to a manger to save us.

Incarnation is "the act whereby the eternal Son of God, the Second Person of the Holy Trinity, without ceasing to be what he is, God the Son, took into union with himself what he before that

1. *Merriam-Webster*, s.v. "incarnation."

act did not possess, a human nature."[2] It's important to clarify that the human nature Jesus possessed is different from our human nature in only one respect—Jesus' humanity does not include sin or his ability to sin. While Jesus was unable to sin, we are unable *not* to sin; there's the huge difference between us and Jesus of Nazareth. Our ability not to sin comes about only through the redemptive work of Jesus' cross. Our analysis begins by selecting various nuances for the incarnation from Scripture followed by Bonhoeffer's interpretation of the incarnation. We conclude by answering two key questions using biblical data and Bonhoeffer's writing: first, "What did the incarnation mean for God?" and second, "What does the incarnation mean for us, today?"

Biblical Data for the Incarnation

A few decades after the resurrection of Jesus Christ, his sayings and ministry were put into belief statements. The Apostles John and Paul have offered the church a biblical basis for the incarnation. We've already mentioned the key biblical statement from John, who wrote late in the first century: "The Word became flesh and made his dwelling among us." This statement pertains to a wonderfully mysterious transformation and tells us how God lives in his people. We now analyze this key text along with others from both the Gospels and the Epistles.

The Word Became Flesh

It is helpful to ask ourselves two questions when doing theology: Who is God and What has he done? We need only go back to the beginning of John's Gospel to understand *who* the Word is as the preexistent eternal Son of God, the Second Person of the Trinity. As mysterious as the virgin birth is, we know that what occurred in Mary's young body resulted in God's birth on earth. All the divinity that Jesus possessed occurred in the Virgin Mary's body.

2. Elwell, *Evangelical Dictionary of Theology*, 601.

The baby she delivers and lays in a manger is no less than the pre-existent Son of God, the Second Person of the Trinity. But he is more. Added to his divinity is the same flesh Adam had when God created a man in his image from the dust of the earth. Adam was made in the image of God from dirt. The incarnation states that Jesus was God and that Jesus was human. He became like us so we could become like him. Jesus of Nazareth is unique among all the gods ever offered by any global religion.

He is God. He is human. He exists as one person with two natures. As such between his birth to his exit from earth, he walks the planet incognito. He wears the masks of a Jewish Galilean carpenter's son and rabbi while being God at the same time. How he appears is the opposite of who he really is.

And Dwelt Among Us

What had God done? The Word lived among his people as God always has. Literally, we translate this phrase, "and tabernacled among us."[3] It's useful to compare the tabernacle with the temple.

Of course, we know about the tabernacle from the Old Testament as the transient place of worship for the wandering children of Israel. God regularly visited and led his people by his glory in a cloud during daylight and a pillar of fire at night. All offerings to Jehovah were made in the tabernacle, the location for the people's forgiveness and healing. A pitched tent is never permanent; its stakes are pounded into the ground only to be pulled up again. So the incarnation reminds that Jesus did not come to earth permanently. He would eventually pull up stakes and travel back to the Father. When Israel became a nation with a king it got a temple. God gave them what they wanted. Kings and a temple proved to be the beginning of the spiritual downfall of Israel. The people wanted to be more like other nations than worship God. While the temple was beautiful and more permanent than the tabernacle, it was destroyed around AD 70 by the Romans. We don't know what

3. Brown and Comfort, *New Greek-English Interlinear New Testament*, 318.

happened to the tabernacle, but we do know that no enemy ever destroyed it.

Jesus wore another mask when he spoke of destroying the temple where he himself "became" the destroyed and rebuilt temple as a metaphor for his death and resurrection. No one knew what he was talking about when he talked about destroying the temple only to rebuild it in three days. This blasphemy resurfaced at his trial and the cross. One impact of this controversial statement implied that even the temple was now temporary. Jesus would now be the temple of God. With Jesus as the raised temple, the people of God once again resumed their pilgrim existence on earth apparently without God's physical presence. However, the church replaced Jesus on earth and now *it* became the temple of God. The Apostle Paul reminds us that our body is the temple of the Holy Spirit who is in us. The author of Hebrews reminds the church that we have no permanent dwelling on earth. As the people of God we are encouraged to have a tent mentality about existence on earth always looking ahead to the eternal city.

To summarize, we find with the incarnation a culmination of God's presence on earth. He fulfills what the tabernacle and the temple anticipated. The church is God's final mask. In his letters to the church, John offers an important standard for assessing genuine spirituality.

Spirits Who Acknowledge That Jesus Came in the Flesh Are from God

John lets us know that Jesus was from the beginning. Then he informs us of what Jesus of Nazareth did as God in the flesh. This verse talks about a word used a lot today—spirituality. Spirituality in and of itself does not make Jesus Christ necessary. There are lots of misguided spirits in the world today which have nothing to do with Christianity. John lets us know that this issue is twenty centuries old. People often say, "I'm spiritual, not religious." This statement says nothing about Jesus or God. In the final days of the first century John warned the church about false spirituality and provided the incarnation as the acid test. You see, John knew that he didn't say in his Gospel, "The Word became spirit." Had God arrived as spirit, who would have known or seen him? When God arrived as a human being, John talked about Jesus as one who the disciples had heard, seen, looked at, and touched. Without going into it, beware of the term Gnostic anytime you see it. That's the name for a false spirituality masking as Christianity. The standard for evaluating spirits in our twenty-first-century culture is the same as in the first century. An incarnational church worships a baby who cried when he was hungry, soiled, or tired just like any baby. Along with John's robust discussion of the incarnation, the Apostle Paul interprets the incarnation in several of his letters.

Jesus Was a Descendant of David

The Gospel of Matthew begins with the genealogy of Jesus Christ as the son of David going back to Abraham. Matthew was Jewish and wrote to a Jewish audience. It would be important for him to lift up Jesus' Jewish religion and culture. By the time Jesus was healing and teaching in the synagogue, virtually everyone knew he was the son of Joseph. Why then on several occasions do people cry out "Son of David" when they see Jesus. For the answer, we turn to the Old Testament where Samuel, the prophet, hears from his colleague Nathan that David will begin a kingdom which lasts forever. This prophecy is clarified and identified with the incarnation later in Isaiah's prophecy about a child who will sit on David's throne, whose government will have no end. Finally, Jeremiah lends support to Son of David as a messianic title speaking of future days when "a righteous Branch, a King will be called: The Lord our Righteousness."[4] Mother Mary was assured that her son would be a king in the line of David.

Paul affirms Jesus' Jewish identity and yet, as a Jew, takes the early faith beyond the limits of Judaism. The Son of God wasn't born into some earthly neutral God-culture. Jesus had Jewish

4. Jeremiah 23:5, 6.

parents, was dedicated according to Jewish law, was schooled in the Torah and joined in the annual pilgrimage to Jerusalem for Passover. What's significant about Christianity is that while culturally Jewish, Jesus makes several moves in his ministry to reach out beyond Judaism. His conversation with a Samaritan women sets the stage for Peter's vision that all humanity is loved by God. Of course, the Apostle Paul follows this precedent when he speaks of the church which is without racial, class, or gender boundaries.

While spawned within Judaism, there is nothing inherently sacred about the Hebrew language for communicating the gospel, just because Jesus was Jewish. The validity of Christianity rests on its residence in any culture spoken in all languages in the global village. This is the miracle of Pentecost. Here the message of human salvation was spoken in all known languages without loss of sanctity or spiritual power. But it all starts with the incarnation, where Jesus, though born Jewish, speaks on behalf of all human beings born into any culture. God arrived as a male, but had a thriving ministry among women. God was Jewish, but spoke with a Samaritan. God was holy, but had dinner with a tax collector. The church has taken God's place on earth. He expects us to be his presence among all people. To do so often requires leaving privileges behind to be humble. The incarnation means that a descendant of David, God's Son, became a son of humanity.

Appearing in Human Likeness, God Humbled Himself

Thus far John and Matthew have offered nuances related to the incarnation which pertain to the nature and person of Jesus, his life among us, a test for true spirituality and his Jewish culture as the unique God-human. In this section we turn to Paul for further aspects of the incarnation.

In his letter to the church in Philippi he speaks of Jesus Christ as one who did not hang onto his celestial privileges, but gave them up to be a servant. God didn't need to become human. Jesus never needed to have lived as the unique God-human being. The Trinity as Father, Son and Holy Spirit had a happy life in community with one another. The thrust of this text is the grace of God extended to humanity in the choice God made to save his creation through Jesus Christ. There is no logic behind going from throne to manger, from rich to poor, or from privilege to humility. Only sheer grace explains what appearing as a human being cost God. He was under no obligation to do so. This is the ironic scandal of the gospel. The incarnation conveys God's willingness to give up his honor and privilege to become like us.

He Appeared in a Body as a Mystery of Godliness

This is the only text in Scripture which explicitly refers to the incarnation as a mystery of godliness. The Gospels speak succinctly of the incarnation as a matter of fact. Matthew simply states how the birth of Jesus came about. Jesus' birth is linked to the Old Testament prophecies which are especially important for his Jewish audience. Matthew addresses Joseph, yet it is within Mary's body that the incarnation takes place. Matthew mentions nothing about the mystery of Mary's supernatural pregnancy by the Holy Spirit. Mark mentions nothing about the incarnation. Luke is the only Gospel author who uses *virgin* when referring to Mary. She's concerned about God's mysterious method to create life within her body. An angel reminds Mary about Elizabeth's unique pregnancy. Mary accepts by faith the mystery of what God might be doing by agreeing to God's awkward plan. In so doing, she models for all of future disciples the life of faith required to accept all the unknowns of following Jesus as Lord. We've located in the Gospels and Epistles nuances from several authors regarding the incarnation. Interpretations have spanned the waterfront from matter-of-fact statements to unexplainable mysteries of God. The incarnation asserts that God willingly humbled himself to take on human flesh, mysteriously conceived as the son of a young mother. Having analyzed key texts for the incarnation from Scripture, we now turn to Dietrich Bonhoeffer's radical interpretation of the manger.

Bonhoeffer's Theological Interpretation of the Manger

Bonhoeffer points out a significant difference between the incarnation and the incarnate one. Simply stated, the former term relates to the *how* of the virgin birth. But the latter term refers to the *who* as the glorified God in human form. He emphasizes the latter over the former. It is the trinitarian God who is seen as the incarnate one. The issue of the incarnation is the glorification of God. For Bonhoeffer, what is at stake when God became human is not so much an answer to the mysterious question "How is he?" but "Who is he?"[5] With this emphasis on the Incarnate One, any notion of being spiritual-only is eliminated. Bonhoeffer's theology stresses the concrete and visible, not the abstract and invisible. Of course, he gets this from Luther, whose robust theology of the cross is defined by calling a thing what it is. We see God in the feeding trough; not some *idea* of divinity. *God* is in that manger!

Bonhoeffer's insists that neither humiliation nor exaltation alters the fact that the infant in the manger is wholly God and wholly human. Nothing about a crying, hungry, tired baby reveals the divine. He makes none of the divine properties evident in his humble birth, yet claims that his baby is God. How God appears has nothing at all to do with who God is. "He is veiled in the hiddenness of scandal."[6] Bonhoeffer's allusion to scandal here permeates his entire theology. An infant body is another of God's masks. He finds in Luther's hidden-revealed concept that God reveals himself in his opposite. The baby in the manger appears to be anything but God. In his humiliation, we behold his glory. Later, we will address how the manger anticipates the cross. Suffice it to say here Bonhoeffer finds a mutuality between the manger and the cross.

The awkward events of the incarnation surface the scandal of Jesus' birth and the shame it brought upon Joseph, Mary, and their respective families. But in that scandal we observe both intervention and faith. God intervenes and two bewildered young

5. Bonhoeffer, *Christ the Center*, 104–5.
6. Ibid., 106.

parents on earth demonstrate faith. We see that God works in truly mysteriously ways as a matter of course, even if it involves scandal. We'll later see how scandal also permeates a theology of the cross and tomb. The more we realize the scandal, the more we discover and appreciate God's grace.

Applying Bonhoeffer's theology of the incarnation offers us guidelines for Christian living. "God is not ashamed of the lowliness of human beings. God is near to lowliness, he loves the lost, the neglected, the unseemly, the excluded, the weak and broken."[7] Because he arrives in such low estate, God can sympathize with the marginalized. Bonhoeffer lifts up our need for mystery: "A human life is worth as much as the respect it holds for the mystery."[8] Here he urges us to get beyond what can be calculated in order to embrace mystery in our life like a child. Both Luther and Bonhoeffer speak of the Incarnate One as a beggar. Luther would say Jesus comes to earth incognito, the one revealed in his hiddenness. Matthew provides the basis for Luther's notion of Jesus as beggar in the parable of the sheep and goats. Here Jesus actually *is* neighbor who is sick, hungry, or in prison. The application is clear: we are to treat any other human being as Christ's sister or brother. Their demand on us is God's demand to love them as we love ourselves; that way others will know we love God with all our heart, strength, and mind. One of Bonhoeffer's signature phrases is his often-misunderstood religion-less Christianity. This idea is rooted in his view of the manger. "No priest, no theologian stood at the manger of Bethlehem. And yet all of Christian theology has its origin in the wonder of all wonders: that God became human."[9] In other words, nothing religious happened around the manger when God was born to Mary. Only ordinary people, shepherds and a poor mother and confused father, were there. While theologically profound, the incarnation has nothing to do with perfunctory or rote religion. No teacher of the law, temple official, ruler of a synagogue showed up at the manger, even though they

7. Bonhoeffer, *God Is in the Manger*, 16.

8. Ibid.

9. Ibid., 28.

all had access to the Law and Prophets, which predicted Messiah's birth. Herod's murderous jealousy of Jesus the baby outweighed any interest religious people had in who lay in the manger. "The lowly God-human is the scandal of pious people."[10] The religious wanted signs, wonders, and miracles. But it is the humility of the manger which anticipates Jesus' puzzling responses to all requests for miracles. Therein lies the scandal; for had Jesus diverted interest in his mystery by performing miracles, faith would be extraneous. People would have believed in the miracles; that is, in only what they could see. But this is not faith. Belief in a supernatural act cannot be faith in God. So the scandal of the manger is how it disrupts the pious and the religious with purposeful ambiguity and enigmatic responses. For Bonhoeffer it is the beginning of a religion-less Christianity where only those who obey, believe; and only those who believe, obey. Religion requires neither belief nor obedience. Following Jesus does.

Finally, Bonhoeffer's view of the incarnation provides a radical view of what it means to be human. "Human beings become human because God became human."[11] Throughout this chapter we've focused on the Word becoming flesh. We've seen the vast difference of being only God to becoming Jesus, the God-human. But what might it mean for us, already human beings, to become human? Among the last things he wrote, Bonhoeffer pondered what it might mean to be religionless Christians; it was his way of saying that Christians needed to be less pious and more incarnational; that is, to be human. "How do we go about being 'religionless worldly Christians' without understanding ourselves as privileged but as belonging to the world?"[12] Note how his thought parallels Paul's thought on the incarnation regarding Jesus Christ giving up the privileges of heaven. For our purposes, we equate becoming human with becoming this-worldly Christians.

Bonhoeffer takes us back to the Garden of Gethsemane. He speaks of religion as a withdrawal into pious feelings rather than

10. Ibid., 52.

11. Bonhoeffer, *Letters and Papers from Prison*, 364.

12. Ibid., 480.

dealing objectively with reality. In the garden, Jesus wanted only companionship during his loneliness pain. His closest followers failed him. "The human being is called upon to share in God's suffering at the hands of a godless world."[13] That is, the Christian knows what it means to be part of the church, a scandalous community of human beings. The Christian realizes what the Apostle Paul called that unified new humanity, the church. Bonhoeffer grasps the church and the individual Christian as radically human just as Jesus was. The Christian who is becoming human lives a sacramental life, by being broken bread and poured out wine for the neighbor. The human Christian runs toward the suffering of the other; she stays awake with Jesus in Gethsemane. When others flee the cross, she remains like Mary Magdalene did at the feet of Jesus Christ during his deepest suffering on a cross.

Bonhoeffer says that to believe in Christ is to be there *for others*, just as Jesus was. Bonhoeffer defines the church as being itself only when it is *for others*. Of course, this notion is rooted in his vicarious representative for humanity where now becoming human means coming alongside the neighbor *for her, on her behalf, as her advocate*. "The church is church only when it is for others."[14] Participation is a huge word for Bonhoeffer. Within the context of becoming the human being Christ creates in us, he says this: "It is not the religious act that makes someone a Christian, but rather participating in God's suffering in the worldly life."[15] Here is a radical notion. Not one which is only spiritual, but one which is primarily incarnational.

Bonhoeffer, like Christ often did in the Gospels, stands the common religious wisdom on its head as he pleads for the church to become human. He urges us to be human by being this-worldly. That is, to become the opposite of the narcissism abounding in our self-absorbed culture. In this section, we've discussed Bonhoeffer's theological perspectives on the incarnation symbolized by a manger. We've noted his use of scandal to describe the incarnation.

13. Ibid., 501.
14. Ibid., 503.
15. Ibid., 480.

Conclusion

What did the incarnation mean for God? It meant descent. It meant loss of status. It meant the loss of all privileges associated with royalty. It meant poverty after knowing a life of wealth. It meant downsizing from a castle to homelessness. It meant humiliation. It meant being consistently misunderstood by parents, neighbors, synagogue leaders, and disciples. It meant living with the scandalous suspicions of an awkward birth story. It meant giving up eternal permanence in a joyful relationship with two other members of the Trinity interrupted by the conflicts and pains of earthly existence as a human being. It meant being called a blasphemer. It meant watching the desecration of your Father's house, the temple. It meant listening to so-called religious leaders misquote your words and then being criticized for correcting them. In sum, there was nothing in it for God that he had not already possessed. Jesus gained nothing by saving us.

What does the incarnation mean for us, today? Everything. We have only to gain because God became human; we have nothing to lose. By grace, we got what we *didn't* deserve; in mercy, we didn't get what we *did* deserve. God even provided the faith we need to believe all of it. We gained access to the Father through Jesus the God-human. Without the manger, we would not have known God. Because of the incarnation, we've seen, heard, and touched God. Mary held God in her arms. Fishermen heard his Sermon on the Mount. A leper felt Jesus' touch and was healed. Thomas touched Jesus' wounds and believed.

Because God became human, we were given the hope that God understands us as weak human beings. God experienced every pain and wound imaginable for humanity. All this began among the warmth of animals during a cold night in a manger. God was born in Bethlehem, the house of bread. The words for the bread "This is my body" from the Eucharist got its meaning from the city of God's birth. The Prophets stated, "*For unto you* a child is born, *unto you* a son is given." The all-important gift of God *for us and with us* begins as we wait expectantly during Advent, just like the expectant virgin. No wonder we give gifts to one another at Christmas. God gave his only son at the incarnation. The infant in that manger was the Redeemer, Savior, and Lord of the world! That's who was in it *for us!*

Chapter 7

Redemption: Victory over Sin

IN THE LAST CHAPTER we talked about the incarnation as a theological interpretation of the manger. We surveyed biblical nuances and analyzed Bonhoeffer's views of Christ's birth, concluding with questions related to its meaning for both God and humanity.

In this chapter we interpret the cross as redemption. We'll survey several biblical texts. To enhance readability, only general reference to individual texts will be made as either from the Gospels or the Epistles. We'll get into a theological interpretation of bread, wine, and the cross. Finally, we'll analyze Bonhoeffer's theology of the cross.

We assert that the work of Jesus Christ on the cross provides humanity with the capability to have *victory and power over sin*. Literally, *redemption* is "the act of buying something back."[1] Economically, this is unusual. Typically, we buy something once and keep it. But we lost what God intended for humanity, which was to know only God and to know only what's good. The entrance of sin into creation left us knowing good and evil, making the death of Jesus Christ necessary. Because of the cross, we can be restored to God's original intention for us. The image of God given at creation, but tainted by sin, may now be restored to the image of the crucified Christ. We now possess the power of the

1. *Merriam-Webster*, s.v. "redemption."

Holy Spirit with the capability to know only God. The work of Jesus Christ on the cross for our salvation reclaims persons previously estranged from God because of sin. Redemption means God repurchases us along with all of his creation. Humanity is reinstated to its original position as created in the image of God devoid of the penalty and power of sin, though sin's presence remains. To summarize, redemption is the costly gracious act of a dying God on a cross for sin and sinners. Given an emphasis upon purchase, price, and cost, we now survey several appropriate texts providing nuanced meanings for redemption.

We will investigate both the Gospels and the Epistles of the New Testament to discover nuanced explanations of redemption. The Gospels chart the life, sayings, and ministry of Jesus of Nazareth. The Epistles, largely written by the Apostle Paul, interpret the words and events of Jesus' life from which we derive the teachings of the church. The Gospels aren't doctrinal; the Epistles don't quote Jesus. Taking the two together provides a robust view of our redemption.

Biblical Data for Redemption

Jesus never refers explicitly to his cross in any of the Gospels. Nowhere in the Gospels is Jesus ever quoted as explicitly linking his death on a cross with redemption. The key here is the absence of his *explicit* use of words; for he does use synonyms and related concepts to describe his work of salvation which anticipate his crucifixion and suffering. It is not unlike Jesus to be enigmatic about his ministry on earth. Here we consider Jesus' statements which allude to the role of the cross for the forgiveness of sin from both the Gospels and the Epistles.

Jesus Said That He Must Suffer, Be Killed and on the Third Day Be Raised to Life

Here we have the well-known encounter with Peter, who challenges Jesus' prediction of his suffering and death. There is no way at this time that Peter could have possibly connected Jesus' death on a cross for the forgiveness of sin. Clearly, in this text Jesus makes no such connection. Jesus makes no mention of why he will die. He doesn't speak of any relationship of his death to the forgiveness of sin. He says nothing about dying on a cross. Later in this passage, Jesus speaks of the cross, but it's the cross his disciples will take up. Peter's objection has two possible explanations. First, his love for Jesus can't imagine anything good about Jesus suffering, dying, and rising from the dead. Jesus' words sound depressing to him. In fact, today we would take such words seriously as coming from someone who is not safe to himself. Jesus sounds morbid and depressed. Second, if Jesus must die, why? If he's to continue leading a renewal movement within Judaism, how would his suffering and dying help the cause? In the next text, we find Jesus telling his purpose for coming to earth.

For the Son of Man Came to Seek and to Save the Lost

This is one of Jesus' few statements regarding redemption. The context for this statement is the familiar story of the tax collector, Zacchaeus. We note that Jesus numbers him among those Jews with Abraham's faith, even though fellow Jews number Zacchaeus among the sinners. Ironically, Jesus speaks of saving the lost, which includes sinners, not the so-called religious who can't yet admit that they really are sinners. We note that in this text no personal decision of faith is stated in so many words about Zacchaeus' belief in Jesus as Messiah. We're told about his acts of repentance to restore money to those he's cheated and also to the poor in general. Zacchaeus may have made faith statements about Jesus as Messiah; Luke simply doesn't record it and prefers to highlight the acts of repentance rather than words of belief. Finally, in our day much has been said about so-called "seekers" looking for God. Here we find that the true seeker is the Son of Man, Jesus Christ, seeking the lost just like God did in the garden when he looked for a hiding Adam and Eve. Lost sheep don't go looking for their shepherd; rather the shepherd leaves the flock to find that one sheep who has left the fold. So far we've discussed Jesus' death to save lost persons. This final Gospel text is taken from the Last Supper where the symbols of Christ's death are first introduced.

And the Son of Man Will Be Handed Over to Be Crucified

This is the only recorded statement where Jesus speaks explicitly about the cross. It contains no explicit linkage to redemption or salvation. It merely states how he will die. Jesus is speaking to his disciples about the Passover and without taking a breath happens to mention that he will be crucified! Later, during the Passover meal Jesus speaks of the cup of his blood as a new covenant poured out for the forgiveness of sins. He makes no explicit connection of this new act within the Passover dinner and his pending crucifixion.

Not until Peter's Pentecost sermon does the New Testament reader receive an interpretation of Jesus' crucifixion linked with repentance and the forgiveness of sins; that is, with redemption. It is only after the resurrection that the separate statements by Jesus during his life are now integrated into a formal teaching. That is, Jesus will suffer, die, and be raised from the dead as the culmination of seeking the lost by dying on a cross for the forgiveness of sins. Now that we've looked into Jesus' actual words, we go to the Epistles where the Apostle Paul interprets the anthropology of suffering and death on a cross as redemption from sin.

Redemption Came by Jesus Christ as a Sacrifice of Atonement through His Blood

Just over two decades after Jesus' death and resurrection, the Apostle Paul wrote a letter to the church in Rome. Here we have some of the earliest statements linking Jesus' death on a cross with redemption. This paragraph offers one of the most robust statements of the gospel in the Bible. Paul's broader theme is the righteousness of God. He also speaks of atonement. Atonement is associated with offering a sacrifice to remove sin. John the Baptizer spoke of Jesus as the Lamb of God sacrificed for sinners. This idea from the Law and the Prophets would have resonated with any Jewish person. The Old Testament mentions many required sacrifices to atone for sin. John tells us that Jesus is the *only* required sacrificial Lamb who offers forgiveness of sin. Paul compares the uniqueness of Christ's sacrifice to the Old Testament's multiple sacrifices in this truth-laden text. He continues on the theme of the cross and redemption later in his letter, speaking of being justified by his blood. Here's an explicit linkage of the cross with redemption using two new but related words: justified and reconciled. The former is a legal term involving acquittal from breaking the law; the latter, a term of healing for a broken relationship. Both terms are part of the overall process of redemption.

We Preach Christ Crucified as Our Righteousness, Holiness, and Redemption

The message of the gospel is *Christ crucified*, not Christ resurrected. From the manger to the grave, Jesus' life is one scandal after another. God is born in a feeding trough. God is buried in a borrowed tomb where it was rumored his body was stolen to explain why it was empty. The scandal of the cross is that God is nailed to its wood as a criminal. While the incarnation and resurrection are indispensable to redemption, the Apostle Paul insists that the core message of the gospel is *Christ crucified*. That's what the earliest disciples proclaimed to begin the Christian faith. That message was ludicrous! It was mocked by the Jews who wanted miracles; it was scorned by intelligent Greeks who thought the whole thing was foolish. Scandal is the gospel's strength, wisdom, and power. God could have saved the world more rationally. He could have arrived as a persuasive orator before huge public rallies, proclaiming salvation through belief in him as the way back to God. World redemption might have been the result of a massive military victory by God as a conquering general. But in the gospel we find only illogic, irrationality, and weakness. How could suffering and dying as a criminal offer salvation? Yet that's precisely what the Apostle

Paul says is our message: that an abandoned, rejected, and dying Jesus of Nazareth is the way for us to become right with God! No wonder to believe in God's grace requires faith! And such faith comes only from God who gives it to us! It is a scandalous Christ who buys us back to make us whole.

God Made Him Sin That We Might Become the Righteousness of God

This is the most radical statement about redemption in the Bible. It defies explanation. It remains the great mystery of our salvation. How are we to conceive of God making Jesus sin? This is an inherent contradiction! God doesn't make anyone or anything sin. Then why does he do this to his own Son? More scandal; more mystery. But, this is God's grace! We *can* conceive of Jesus Christ bearing *our sin*; then, we're asked to grasp Christ bearing the *sin of the whole world!* We've seen enough cinema accounts of Jesus enduring punishment for our sin. While difficult to look at, we have an idea of what it cost God to bear our sin. But when it comes to this verse, where we're actually challenged to believe that *God equated Jesus with sin*; it's more than any human being can imagine. There is no way to explain how God becomes sin. It is the greatest scandal of the gospel! When you read this verse, think of the infant in the manger who will become sin for your salvation. At the same time, think about grace, and you'll see why it's so amazing. Luther spoke economically of this happy exchange whereby humanity gets God's righteousness by giving him its sin. This verse summarizes Bonhoeffer's insistence that Christ dies on our behalf as the vicarious representative for the world.

In Him We Have Redemption through His Blood, the Forgiveness of Sins

Here, redemption, the cross, and forgiveness of sins are explicitly integrated. We have redemption through his blood. God has bought us back through the suffering and death of Jesus Christ. This is what the cross means for us. Paul lists this profound truth within a litany of praise for all our spiritual blessings in Christ. Jesus mentioned the cup of his blood during the Last Supper as a new covenant. Here Paul theologically interprets those words for the diverse Jewish-Gentile church at Ephesus. The shedding of blood was always required to cleanse Israel from sin. In the transition from Passover to the Lord's Supper, Jesus anticipates the fulfillment of John the Baptist's statement: "Look, over there, the Lamb of God who takes away the sin of the world!" Our status before a holy God is changed for the better because of Christ's work on the cross. A consequence of our changed status is the forgiveness of our sins. A challenge that accompanies the consequence is that we do for others what Christ did for us; that is, we keep on forgiving one another! When in doubt, show grace and mercy. Bonhoeffer's economic analogy is this: What cost God so much cannot be cheap for us. Clearly, becoming a curse sustains the scandal of the cross.

Christ Redeemed Us from the Curse of the Law by Becoming a Curse for Us

Recall our ethnographic analysis of how hanging from a tree was God's curse for a sin punishable by death. Theologically, that Jesus hung from a tree as one nailed to a cross scandalizes the death of Jesus Christ. That is, because Jesus became the curse, you and I don't have to endure the same punishment. God did that for us. Just as Christ became sin for us he also becomes a curse for us. In each case, Jesus Christ operates as our vicar as one who pleads our case before God the Judge. Christ becomes our defense attorney, our advocate before the Father. Or, as Paul tells his understudy Timothy, Christ is the only mediator between God and humanity, the human being who is Christ Jesus. Both sin and its curse lose all their power over us at the cross of Jesus. The cross is our victory over both the power and penalty of sin.

No New Testament author has claimed that the cross removes the presence of sin. In fact, John states that we're liars if we deny sin's presence in us. To repeat, the cross *does* offer victory over both the power and penalty of sin. Jesus buys us back so we need not endure the curse of the law which can only accuse us, but is powerless to save us. The wider context surrounding this Pauline statement speaks of the Holy Spirit who empowers us to live by faith. The law and its curse cannot provide the faith to believe the promised Holy Spirit. Through Christ's cross, both Jews and Gentiles receive the promise of the Holy Spirit by faith. As we appropriate God's grace by faith to ourselves, we become children of God. The once-for-all act of Jesus' cross is necessary and sufficient for our redemption.

Christ Appeared Once for All to Do Away with Sin by the Sacrifice of Himself

The author of Hebrews asserts the superiority of Jesus Christ over Moses, priests, and angels to his largely Jewish Christian audience. The context of this statement compares how the necessary and sufficient power of Christ's blood replaces blood rituals for atonement. When Jesus spoke of the cup of his blood as a new covenant during the Last Supper, he was thinking of the annually repeated priestly sprinkling of blood to cleanse the tabernacle, for without bloodshed, no forgiveness of sins exists. What the priest had to do annually for the people with the blood of animals, Jesus Christ has done *once for all* with his own blood. The Lamb of God who takes away the sin of the world fulfilled all the variations of blood sacrifice in the old covenant. The Old Testament priests annually entered a holy place in the tabernacle called the holy of holies; Jesus entered heaven itself to appear before God as our mediator and advocate. He is there today pleading our case to God on our behalf. This statement is an excellent summary of the new covenant, connecting redemption with the atoning work of Jesus Christ's blood shed on a cross. Paul's letters show how Jesus' enigmatic words about destroying the temple connect the cross to redemption through his blood. We see this same connection in the Apostle John's letters.

The Blood of Jesus Christ, God's Son, Cleanses Us from All Sin

The Apostle John's letters to churches in the province of Asia summarizes the impact of the incarnation upon the gospel. John recalls the words from his Gospel about the Word becoming flesh. This letter affirms Jesus' humanity, who he claims the disciples saw, heard, and touched. His vocabulary is also consistent with how previous New Testament authors speak of redemption. *Christ's blood removes sin's power* is the clear message. The letter relates how a healthy Christian community deals with sin by first not denying it, second by confessing it, and finally by receiving the healing forgiveness of Christ, which restores the church to fellowship with the Father and with his Son, Jesus Christ. Christ's shed blood cancels the power of sin.

In sum, we've analyzed how several New Testament authors have interpreted Jesus' statements linking the cross with redemption. What Jesus implied, these authors have made explicit. We've discovered how Jesus' puzzling words about his death imply he's the Lamb of God who forgives sin. In the next section, we offer a theological interpretation of bread, wine, and the cross.

A Theological Interpretation of Bread, Wine, and the Cross

Our earlier anthropology of bread, wine, and the cross spoke of the ordinariness of the elements of the Eucharist. We noted that bread and wine don't simply appear, but that a process of taking raw materials is involved to produce each. A theological view of the process of baking flour and fermenting grapes suggests important discoveries of Jesus Christ as redeemer. Recall the words heard during the Communion ceremony. As the priest holds up and breaks the bread and pours the wine, she says, "This is my body. . . . This is my blood." Recall how we spoke of the manger as a feeding trough in Bethlehem, which means a house of bread. Here we see how that anthropology anticipates theology. At the time of the Last Supper, Jesus didn't explicitly link these words with the cross. Making bread in the first century involved sifting chaff from the wheat and then using huge millstones to grind the wheat into flour, then mixing with water, yeast, and other ingredients to bake in an oven.

What has this process to do with redemption? The theological parallel here is what we might consider as preparing Jesus' body for sacrifice. His life and ministry involved an initial uprooting from heaven to earth. Just as Jesus told Peter about being sifted like wheat, so also Jesus was sifted while being tempted by Satan, enduring challenges by the religious establishment, dealing with deliverance of evil spirits and tolerating misunderstanding by both family and his closest followers. The last week of his life was extremely painful, with increasingly unbearable suffering, demeaning, mocking, and ultimately crucifixion on a cross. This may be considered the grinding process of converting kernels of wheat into flour. The extreme heat of an oven symbolizes Jesus' trial by fire throughout the slow process of dying. Certainly, bread is a suitable symbol for "This is my body." A similar step-by-step process of picking grapes, separate the pulp from the liquid with a winepress, and placing the juice in a wineskin to ferment over time parallels Jesus' life as described with the bread. Recall the extreme agony Jesus felt in the Garden of Gethsemane. Jesus truly felt life being squeezed out of him, not unlike how an olive press squeezes out oil. We also find the above metaphor useful to imagine what it may mean to participate in the body and blood of Christ. But what might such a participation have to do with making bread and wine?

The liturgical act of participating in the Eucharist continues after the Sunday worship service. The work in the worship service involves only getting up from a pew and returning to your seat. Just as the bread is broken and the wine poured out into cups for distribution, the liturgy of the Eucharist continues as the church scatters into ordinary living among others within the community of the church, family, the neighbor, friends, and colleagues at work. Just as the gathered church participates in Communion by consuming bread and wine, it leaves the building as a living sacrament in relationship with others. Jesus, the only real sacrament, models for us what it means to be a "living sacrament" as he related to the infected/paralyzed, those possessed by evil spirits, the dying, the dead, tax collectors, religious leaders, his parents, and disciples. Often there was conflict to be resolved, just like within the church today.

As living sacraments we have confession and forgiveness available by the Spirit to reconcile differences among all people no matter what the conflict may be. The Apostle Paul talks about being a living sacrament this way: "I rejoice in what was suffered for you, and I fill up in my flesh what is still lacking in Christ's afflictions for the sake of his body, which is the church."[2] What is lacking is not Christ's finished work on the cross, but that Christ's sufferings continue through the church. We can't take Communion without being prepared to experience what Jesus did in his life and ministry as we take up our cross and follow. The promise of Scripture is not that we will have no pain to endure, but that God will not take the Holy Spirit from us during our pain; that is, Jesus never leaves nor forsakes us. Remember as recipients of bread and wine, we are preachers/proclaimers of the death of Christ. When we eat and drink, we proclaim the Lord's death. As the body of Christ, the church, we continue the sufferings of Jesus Christ, as he did for us, that the world might experience the gospel. A theological perspective derived from the ordinariness of bread, wine, and a cross enriches what it means to follow Jesus in his steps.

That said, we now explore how a theological interpretation of bread, wine, and the cross sets the stage for Bonhoeffer's theology of the cross.

Bonhoeffer's Theology of the Cross

Bonhoeffer's signature statement about the cross is that Jesus is the vicarious representative[3] for all humanity. Theologically, this speaks of *Christ taking the place for sinners on the cross on their*

---

2. Colossians 1:24.

3. Bonhoeffer, *Sanctorum Communio*, 120.

behalf as an advocate before the Father. Traditional views of the cross mention what's been called the penal substitutionary theory of the atonement. Here the focus of Christ's work on the cross is to take our place, to do for humanity what it could not do for itself. Bonhoeffer would say it this way: "In the death of Jesus on the cross God's judgment and wrath are carried out on all the self-centeredness of humanity."[4] He would include Christ's taking our place as the first part of what he means by vicarious representative action. As we've named this chapter "Redemption: Victory over Sin," he speaks of the cross as: "The death of Christ is victory of love over law."[5] Also, on the notion of victory of the cross over sin, he says about the scandal of God on a cross: "Vicarious representative love triumphs on the criminal's cross and thereby sin is overcome."[6] So Bonhoeffer's concept of vicarious representative action includes a substitutionary view of the cross. We deserved to be on the cross. Christ took our place.

But a substitutionary-only atonement fails to embrace the ongoing ministry of Jesus Christ as our constant advocate before God. So Bonhoeffer would say: Yes, Christ took our place once for all on the cross; but also continues to plead our case for ongoing sin as we "work out our salvation with fear and trembling."[7] Further, Bonhoeffer's view has an anthropological component which is not included in the substitutionary theory. Just as Christ is for us as our advocate, the Christian does the same for others, both within and without the church. The new humanity, the church, created by the cross, involves doing for others what Christ has done for us. This is the second part of Bonhoeffer's view of advocacy on behalf of the neighbor. Christ our vicar models how to be a vicarious representative for the neighbor near and far.

A holistic view of the cross includes Christ *taking our place* and *being for us on our behalf.* One half is substitution; the other half, Christ's vicarious representation. Not to include both halves

4. Ibid., 150.
5. Ibid.
6. Ibid.
7. Philippians 2:12.

of the salvific meaning of the cross is to distort the gospel. If only a substitutionary view is proclaimed, the work of the cross is limited. It pertains only to the individual and becomes a form of redemption which does not include the complete righteousness of God for others. Without a communal dimension, I can feel justified in finding it unnecessary to advocate for my sister in Christ or my neighbor. In so doing, I have settled for a selfish view of the cross, caring only for what's in it for me. To illustrate, this distorted cross has only a vertical beam without the wide open arms of God. On the other hand, if I limit the view of the cross to the advocacy of Jesus for humanity, I may avoid the cross altogether. I could be tempted to remove the theological work of Christ as Savior and Lord for the world. It's possible to look only at the life of Jesus of Nazareth and make a case for caring about others in a humanistic way which doesn't include God's redemptive work. This distorted cross has only a horizontal beam hanging in space with no theological support. In either case, I have misrepresented Scripture's teaching about the cross. Finally, a substitutionary view has no implications for the church. If salvation is only for me, why bother to align with a community of sinners who've experienced the joy of forgiveness available in Christ.

Historically, conservative evangelical Christians immersed in the substitutionary theory possess a weak theology of the church. The church is reduced to an aggregate of persons who've made individual decisions for Christ with a minimal theology of community. Liberal mainline Christians, on the other hand, have maximized the anthropological portion of advocacy for the marginalized often to the neglect of the saving work of the cross for sin and sinners. Neither a conservative nor liberal view of the cross adequately represents the person and work of Jesus Christ. The cross is a both-and concept involving anthropology and theology. Theologically, with the cross God offers victory over sin, reconciling all humanity back to himself. Anthropologically, the cross reconciles humanity in relation to one another in a unique community called the church.

Bonhoeffer's notion of reconciliation from the Apostle Paul and Luther is that *the cross makes the church necessary* as a new humanity launched by Jesus Christ, the God-human. A biblical view of the cross mandates the church. So Bonhoeffer's theology of the cross *is* his theology of the church.

Christ bears our sin on the cross. "The law of Christ is to bear the cross."[8] Bonhoeffer finds the phrase *bearing sin* useful for his view of the cross. It's actually possible because of Jesus' death in our place and for us. From the prophet Isaiah, we have both a description of what Jesus endured *in our place* as well as what he bore *for us on our behalf.* "Surely he took up our infirmities and carried our sorrows, was pierced for our transgressions and crushed for our iniquities. The punishment that was upon him brought us peace and by his wounds we are healed."[9] Holistically, the cross deals with the psychological disorders and physical sickness of human beings; that is, our illnesses, sorrow, sin, and anxieties. Because Christ does all of this on the cross, human beings need not feel unique in their sin or sickness. Jesus embraced all of it before we did. What Christ experienced on our behalf provides the hope we need for healing. Here we find yet another improvement to the "in our place only" theory which has nothing to say about healing of the body. To that degree, the substitution-only view of the cross appears to be gnostic; that is, it tacitly views the body as beside the point, assigning value only to the spiritual. Sadly, this view neglects healing of body, mind, and emotion as a vital component of church ministry. Such a church is religious without being incarnational. Or, spiritual without being human.

Just as Bonhoeffer views the cross as God's provision for *victory over sin*, he sees Jesus' crucifixion as life-giving. "The end of all history is Christ on the cross as the murdered Son of God. The human race dies but Christ is alive. The trunk of the cross becomes the wood of life."[10] The trunk of the cross becomes the wood of life— a most interesting metaphor for the salvific work of Jesus Christ.

8. Bonhoeffer, *Discipleship*, 88.

9. Isaiah 53:4–5.

10. Bonhoeffer, *Creation and Fall*, 145–46.

Recall the scandal involving God cursing God by hanging Jesus on a tree. From a Jewish perspective, anyone God cursed would be hung from a tree. From the Roman view, the cross was for the most despicable criminals. In either case, scandal validates the cross. No logic explains the presence of God on the wood of death.

Bonhoeffer likens the cross to the wood of life. Beyond that, he compares the cross to paradise! "What a strange paradise is this hill of Golgotha, this cross, this blood, this broken body. The tree of life, the cross of Christ, the center of God's world that is fallen, but upheld and preserved—that is what the end of the story about paradise is for us."[11] For Bonhoeffer to call the cross the tree of life takes us back to another Tree of Life in the center of the garden of Eden. It stood in the center of the garden right by the Tree of the Knowledge of Good and Evil, the restricted tree. God never told Adam and Eve not to eat of the Tree of Life. The cross would be that Tree of Life whose wood contained the Savior whose body and blood we taste giving life in the Spirit. Just as the original Tree of Life was in the center of the garden of Eden, the cross of Jesus Christ is at the center of a fallen world redeeming it through the grace of God.

Bonhoeffer emphasizes the *public* nature of the cross. The visible suffering and humiliation of the cross are necessary for our salvation. He states that we cannot find the cross of Jesus if we're afraid of going to the place where Jesus may be found, the public death of a sinner. Jesus did not and, I believe, could not have saved us by dying privately of, say, pneumonia with his family around his bed. The point is the *public* suffering and humiliation of the Savior predicted in the Old Testament was fulfilled by a brutal crucifixion. Similarly, the celebration of the Eucharist must be done *publicly* before the congregation; because, the community only includes admitted sinners who know the grace of God's forgiveness. The church is that place where we all realize we're in the same boat. Bonhoeffer maintains that confession is the closest we come to experiencing the *public* humiliation and shame of the cross.

11. Ibid.

"In confession we affirm the cross."[12] Also, he names intercessory prayer as another example of "seeing each other under the cross of Jesus as poor human beings and sinners in need of grace."[13] When we request prayer, we admit our need just as Christ did when he said "I thirst." It was a suffering God, not one devoid of feeling, emotion, or physical need, who died for us in full view. Ironically, Bonhoeffer speaks of a scandalous cross as sacred. "The holiest sign of the presence of God is the cross."[14] How can the scandal of the Second Person of the Trinity dying as a criminal on a Roman tool of torture be sacred? Anthropologically, this makes no sense. Theologically, it is the only hope for our salvation. The cross offers no gray area or wiggle room. "Jesus' cross is the death sentence on the world . . . human beings live under judgment if they despise it, or live toward salvation if they accept it."[15] In his *Ethics*, Bonhoeffer moves from the cross as *holy* to the cross as the *death sentence* on the world. Of course, the cross is holy because God's holiness requires the judgment of the cross on the world while at the same time offering reconciliation to the First Person of the Holy Trinity. Were God not holy, no cross would have been necessary. The death sentence on the world becomes the death sentence for Jesus Christ as our vicarious representative.

During the last year of his life, Bonhoeffer did some of his most radically theological thinking in prison. His view of the cross focused on a key word: *participation*. Flowing from Christ's vicarious representative role on the cross, he urges the Christian to take up her own cross and to "participate in God's powerless sufferings for the world."[16] During Eucharist, we participate in the body and blood of Christ by eating and drinking bread and wine. Bonhoeffer would call a continuing liturgy of Communion a participation in the sufferings of Jesus Christ. A scattered church goes out the door inspired by the Eucharist to participate with a suffering Christ for the world.

12. Bonhoeffer, *Life Together*, 111.

13. Ibid.

14. Bonhoeffer, *Ethics*, 106.

15. Ibid.

16. Bonhoeffer, *Letters and Papers from Prison*, 480–82.

One of Bonhoeffer's final thoughts on the cross involves anthropology. "Jesus is the human being for others as the Crucified One."[17] From Paul, the message of the gospel is Christ crucified. Here he speaks of the Second Person of the Trinity as the Incarnate One who dies on the cross. The vicarious representative is the human being for others. This thought derives from the Apostle Paul's view of the cross as that event which dismantles all divisions among human beings, be they Jewish versus Gentile, black against white, male versus female, or rich against the poor. The divine Crucified One is not religious, but human. Jesus is the Incarnate One as the Crucified One. Bonhoeffer calls Jesus Christ the best example of what it means to be human. As such, when the Christian takes up his cross and follows the Incarnate-Crucified One, he, too, participates in the humanity of Christ for others. Such participation involves active involvement in a vicarious community called the church.

Conclusion

In this chapter we've offered a theological interpretation of bread, wine, and the cross called redemption, God's victory over sin. We located nuances of redemption from several key biblical texts in the Gospels and the Epistles. We found the cross to be the location for seeking Christ as the Son of Man. Paul's Epistles reminded us of the salvific role of the Lamb of God, the message of the gospel as Christ crucified, the mystery of Jesus becoming sin and a curse for us. Next, we proposed a theological interpretation of bread and wine as the body and blood of Christ broken and shed on the cross. Finally, we considered Bonhoeffer's view of the cross where Jesus is the vicarious representative suffering publicly to dismantle the power and penalty of sin. Jesus not only died in our place once, but also continually intercedes on our behalf before the Father. The message of the Christian faith is *Christ crucified*. The power to proclaim it derives from *Christ resurrected*.

17. Ibid., 501.

What did the cross mean for God? It meant humiliation, suffering, torture, and death. It meant God's loss of a son to the point of making him look like an abusive parent. There was nothing in it for God. The most that Jesus received out of the cross was getting back his throne at his Father's right hand. What does the cross mean for us? Everything. It means grace and mercy. It is the grace of getting forgiveness by the vicarious work of Christ for us. It is the mercy of not getting what we did deserve—the penalty of life estranged from God in this life leading to eternal absence of God.

Having dealt theologically with bread, wine, and the cross, we now interpret the symbol of an empty tomb as the power of Christ's bodily resurrection.

Chapter 8

Resurrection: Victory over Death

NO ONE WAITED FOR the resurrection of Jesus Christ. Even though Jesus predicted it, no one really believed it would happen three days after he died. Synagogue officials feared that Jesus' followers would steal the body and say it occurred, so they convinced the Roman governor Pilate to post a guard to lie about it and then cover it up. The disciples' only concern was to preserve Jesus' body. No one expected to see Jesus of Nazareth ever again. We have no record in the Gospels that Jesus' closest followers ever spoke of the possibility of his resurrection. Rather, the male disciples hid in fear that they might be next to be crucified. The female disciples mourned Jesus' death by going to the tomb with spices, only to discover that the tomb was empty and to be told by angels that Jesus had risen from the dead.

The first Christians never proclaimed an empty tomb. They proclaimed a resurrected Jesus. The tomb could have been empty for reasons other than Jesus' resurrection. The disciples *could* have stolen the body. The guards could have hidden Jesus' body so the disciples couldn't steal it to say he came back to life. However unlikely in this case, there are isolated reports of bodies being placed in morgues prematurely while still alive. Historic theories attempting to explain away the resurrection suggest that Jesus was never really dead, that he rolled the stone away and escaped. All theories aside, to this day the body of the late Jesus of Nazareth has not been found.

A major point related to belief in Jesus' resurrection is the larger issue of whether supernatural events occur in space and in time. For many people, only natural events happen historically. A core belief of the Christian faith is that Jesus of Nazareth bodily came back to life as an event of world history. The Gospels are not some imaginative feel-good notion of encouragement to depressed disciples. They contain verifiable, often eyewitness, accounts of Jesus' life, including the reality of his resurrection. Often science is cited to dispute the historicity or actuality of the resurrection. The scientific method of hypothesis, experiment, data collection, conclusion applies only to repeatable events. The bodily resurrection of Jesus occurred only once. So other means of determining its validity need to be decided. This is why the reliability of the Gospel accounts claiming eyewitnesses of many appearances is critical. It's also why the resurrection is beyond the scope of the scientific method's limitations to verify some hypothesis. The resurrection of Jesus Christ was a once-for-all supernatural event validated in space and in time by hundreds of eyewitnesses.

The turning point in world history was when Jesus of Nazareth, with the wounds of crucifixion still on his hands, side, and feet appeared to individuals and groups of people. They spread the word that God had raised him from the dead. He spoke with them, ate with them, and doubters saw and touched his wounds to be assured of his identity. Only days after various appearances of a living Jesus, a fearful, doubting, fledging group of disciples watched the Second Person of the Trinity return to heaven. They received the Holy Spirit, the Third Person of the Holy Spirit, bore witness to his resurrection, and boldly proclaimed the story of Jesus, concluding that he was the anticipated Jewish Messiah. The words Jesus used to launch his ministry parallel the first words of proclamation from Peter to repent and be baptized in the name of Jesus Christ for the forgiveness of your sins.

While Christ crucified is the core message of the gospel, Christ resurrected is Christianity's "major fact in a defense of its teachings. If Jesus didn't literally rise from the dead, then the entire Christian faith is fallacious."[1] Either the entire Bible is false or the resurrection of Jesus of Nazareth is true. We now turn our attention to those biblical texts devoted to Jesus' prediction that he would rise from the dead.

Biblical Data for the Resurrection

While resurrection has Old Testament roots within the Prophets and in the Judaism of Jesus' day, we confine our biblical analysis to the Gospels, Acts, and the Epistles. At the outset it's important to distinguish Christian notions of resurrection from prevailing religions of the day. Greeks held to the idea of resurrection as *immortality of the soul*. Christians believed resurrection as *the raising of the body* mentioned in the New Testament and then in the creeds.

From the Gospels, Jesus' resurrection statements are subtle and cryptic. At the last Passover he celebrated with his disciples, he predicted that his closest followers would deny and leave him. But then he follows it up immediately speaking of his post-resurrection appearances. These words are validated in Jesus' several post-resurrection appearances. Early in his ministry Jesus said, "Destroy the temple, and I will raise it again in three days."[2] The resurrection is the fulfillment of the cryptic "raise it again in three days." These words are brought up as evidence against him at his trial and as an insult at the cross. When Jesus cryptically spoke of his resurrection to his disciples, they missed the point every time.

Further mention of the resurrection in the Gospels comes from others. Ironically, the temple officials paid more attention to the possibility of the resurrection than did Jesus' disciples. It is the Pharisees who urged Pilate to post a guard at the tomb because of Jesus' resurrection predictions. The final resurrection statement in the Gospels is spoken by angels at the tomb to grieving women after Jesus rose from the dead. The church has been quoting these angels ever since.

1. Elwell, *Evangelical Dictionary of Theology*, 1014.
2. Matthew 26:32.

While Jesus' mention that he would rise again is obviously predictive, most interpretation of Christ's resurrection occurs after the fact as the church is launched. The single greatest evidence for the resurrection of Jesus Christ is that a church of human beings who previously denied and fell away from Jesus began proclaiming his rising from the dead! The tomb was still empty, but it was a crucified-resurrected living Jesus who challenged the fledgling followers to remain unified in community. That community was the church. The existence of the church as the living body of Christ on earth remains the most compelling proof of Jesus' resurrection! The resurrection is reenacted every time Christians gather for celebration. The living body of Jesus Christ sings, listens, speaks, eats, and drinks the sacrament and leaves to spread the word!

The initial proclamation of the resurrection was preached by Jesus' chief recovering denier, the Apostle Peter. Its message was twofold. Peter first reminded his audience that Jesus was exalted to the right hand of the God. Then Peter urged his audience to repent for the forgiveness of their sins to receive the gift of the Holy Spirit. It's important to note what Jesus got back by going through his death and resurrection: his exaltation and return to his rightful place in heaven at the right hand of the Father. Humanity received the gift of the Holy Spirit and the forgiveness of its sins. Often, our focus upon ourselves neglects the exaltation of Jesus Christ, the Second Person of the Trinity, as result of the crucifixion and resurrection. God's plan for world redemption involves the exaltation of a humble Savior and the forgiveness of sinners. Recall, however, that Jesus had been exalted for an eternity before coming to earth as a human being, dying as a criminal and rising from the dead. We might say that Jesus was "re-exalted."

In this sermon Peter displays his knowledge of the Psalms and draws an important connection between David's words and Christ's resurrection. Peter treats Psalm 16:8–11 as a prophecy of Christ's resurrection. While speaking to God about himself, he's also forecasting Jesus' bodily rising from the dead. Peter's statement of God raising Jesus from the dead finds its forecast in David's "you will not abandon me to the grave, nor will you let your Holy One see decay."[3] Recall that the only concern among Jesus' disciples was that his body receive sustaining spices as part of a proper Jewish burial. Over time, even the best and greatest quantity of spices would not have prevented decay. God's raising Jesus body from the dead assures a permanent resistance to decomposition. Of course, there's much more to this resurrection than preventing decay. Peter assures his audience that even though Jesus is David's kingly descendant, vast differences exist between Jesus' tomb and David's. As much as the burial and tomb of a Jewish king are important, an alive Jesus surpasses David's tomb and appropriately marginalizes Joseph's garden burial place—a tomb which never again receives any mention in the proclamation of the gospel—empty or occupied.

The themes of early church preaching follow a certain pattern begun with Peter's first sermon. First, there is a linkage to the Old Testament people and events. These early addresses had Jewish audiences which were proclaimed by Jewish disciples. Second, a clear statement of the gospel of Jesus Christ was presented: his life, death, and resurrection. Finally, a response was urged to repent and to be baptized. The results of such preaching were dramatic, often involving mass conversion or landing the disciples in jail, where they continued to proclaim the good news.

From this first sermon by Peter in Acts 2, the remainder of Luke's epistle and the later preaching of Paul evidence how the death and resurrection for the forgiveness of sins and eternal life dominated early church preaching. Just as Peter showed how he would love Jesus by tending his sheep, a converted murderer of early Christians, the Apostle Paul, preached and taught the resurrection.

Paul's letter to the church in Rome offers thorough instruction on the resurrection. The apostle's greeting mentions resurrection, baptism, indwelling of the Holy Spirit, and belief for salvation. Peter proclaimed sermons; Paul taught and applied the resurrection to living the Christian life. The critical nuance from Paul related to resurrection is the role of the Holy Spirit. Right from his greeting

---

3. Psalm 16:10.

he connects the Holy Spirit's power to the proclamation of the gospel. "The Gospel of God regarding his Son through the Spirit of holiness was declared with power to be the Son of God by his resurrection from the dead: Jesus Christ our Lord."[4]

Paul also speaks of resurrection symbolized in baptism. The proclamation of the gospel occurs in the sacrament of baptism, where Christ's death and resurrection are ritualized in the life of the believer within the church community. Parenthetically, this takes us back to anthropology, where within baptism we find an important symbol—water. Paul is careful to delineate the separate roles of the cross and the living Christ. The death of Jesus Christ is God's victory over sin and sins, and the resurrection of Jesus Christ is God's victory over death. In either case, the Christian life mysteriously parallels the death and resurrection of Christ. Christ's death offers us the victory to no longer be addicted to sinning. Christ's death offers us the victory of living new life in the Holy Spirit, anticipating the physical rising of our bodies from our own death. The Apostle states that we don't get new life without dying to sin. First-century Christians began an ongoing ritual of immersion baptism by being placed under water to identify with Christ's death and burial. Then, they were lifted up from under the water to symbolize being raised with Christ.

Paul links the resurrection to the indwelling of the Holy Spirit in the body of the believer. "And if the Spirit of him who raised Jesus from the dead is living in you, he who raised Christ from the dead will also give life to your mortal bodies through his Spirit, who lives in you."[5] While Peter speaks of God raising Jesus from the dead, Paul focuses upon the Holy Spirit as the power behind the resurrection. Of course, there's no contradiction here since the mystery of the Trinity is the Father, Son, and Holy Spirit in constant community. When Jesus spoke of destroying the temple, he was speaking of his body. The Apostle Paul refers to the human body as a temple of the Holy Spirit, who lives inside the believer. Just as the presence of God visited the tabernacle out in

4. Romans 1:1–4.

5. Romans 8:11.

the desert and indwelt the temple, so also the Holy Spirit is present in a Christian's body. It is our identity as followers of Jesus.

Finally, Paul includes the resurrection as part of the confession one makes to identify with Christ as a follower. In one of the most succinct conversion statements to Christians in Rome, Paul talks about what one must say and believe to trust in Jesus Christ. One of the earliest statements of faith is *Jesus is Lord*. It is an announcement that Jesus Christ is Sovereign and King as Creator and Sustainer of the Universe. It proclaims that Jesus of Nazareth is the Yahweh of the Torah, the deity of all Israel. It is the righteousness of God which characterizes the process of world redemption. All this said, we can then say that "Jesus is my personal Savior," for this claim is part and parcel of *Jesus is Lord*. Essentially Paul is talking about what God gets out of the process of salvation compared to what we receive. Recall that Jesus is exalted to the throne of the Father; we are forgiven our sins and given the Holy Spirit. Along with a verbal confession of Jesus' lordship, Paul urges heartfelt belief in the resurrection. When he speaks of the heart, he's employing a holistic view of engagement with body, mind, soul, and spirit. That is, Jesus Christ is the center of life for the Christian.

Paul discusses the resurrection in an entire section of his first letter to the church in Corinth. In it he follows a progression of thought validating Jesus' bodily resurrection and predicting the bodily resurrection of all persons. As previously mentioned, a key tenet of the Christian faith is the bodily resurrection of Jesus Christ. Speaking of Christ's rising from death, he focuses upon the appearances of Jesus to many various persons—even to himself in his dramatic conversion experience while traveling to Damascus. Then he addresses those who continue to doubt that resurrection from death is even possible. George F. Handel's *Messiah* includes a stirring chorus from this passage where Paul compares the entrance of death by Adam to the resurrection from death by Jesus Christ. Just as through crucifixion Christ proclaims victory over sin, so also through resurrection Christ proclaims victory over death. Finally, the Apostle Paul talks about the type of body human beings have in the resurrection. "And just as we have borne the likeness of the earthly man, so shall we bear the likeness of the man from heaven."[6] It is clear that Paul proclaims the reality of Jesus' bodily resurrection and that he believes in the resurrection of all humanity when Christ returns.

Later in the New Testament, there is an assortment of references to the resurrection from Paul, the author of Hebrews, Peter, and John. Each text addresses the power, living hope, and details about how resurrection will take place in the last days. One mysterious text, going back to the Gospels, is curiously omitted in preaching or writing about resurrection. Precisely at the point of Jesus' death, it talks about tombs broken open with the bodies of many holy people who had died raised to life. This is one of the untouchable texts in all of Scripture. Some biblical editors spiritualize it as symbol, making an arbitrary decision not to take it historically, even though they argue for literal translations just about everywhere else! But there is no reason not to take this text historically or literally, no matter how difficult it is to explain. I would also note that this unique resurrection of many bodies is no attempt to "one-up" Christ's resurrection; for these resurrected people went public *only after* God raised Jesus from the dead. No later reference to this awkward event occurs anywhere else in the Bible. No theology of the resurrection seems to require its explanation. Possibly the church is taught here that we need not know everything!

In sum, the biblical nuances for the resurrection span the waterfront from what Jesus said about it for himself, what others said about it prior to its occurrence, and then how the early church interpreted it as a core teaching of the gospel. Using the details from the biblical analysis, we now attempt to interpret the empty tomb.

A Theological Interpretation of an Empty Tomb

Good theology begins with good anthropology. Jesus of Nazareth was not the first person recorded in the New Testament to have risen from the dead—the twelve-year-old daughter of a synagogue

---

6. 1 Corinthians 15:49.

leader was. The proof she was alive was not her empty bed, but that she stood up, walked around, and had something to eat. The second person who came to life after dying was Lazarus. His tomb became empty as he walked out. The proof of his resurrection was this statement: "Martha served, while Lazarus was among those reclining at the table with Jesus."[7] Lazarus had something to eat. Jesus raised both the little girl and his friend Lazarus from the dead. Both the girl and Lazarus would eventually die. Jesus would never die after his resurrection.

The proof of Jesus' resurrection is not an empty tomb. No church would exist because of the proclamation of a vacant tomb. The church came into existence as ordinary human beings spoke, walked with, and ate with the resurrected Jesus of Nazareth. He demonstrated his resurrection by being human. In every one of Jesus' resurrection appearances, one aspect is common to all—it was the ordinary aspects of living which proved the resurrection—physical wounds, talking, walking, and eating.

The resurrection of Jesus remains unique. He was the hidden Second Person of the Trinity in a human being: the Word became flesh. Jesus would never die again. He went from resurrection to ascension back to heaven. Only he had the power of God to raise Jairus' young daughter, Lazarus, and those mysterious holy people from their graves. The historical Christ, the Jesus of faith, was the subject of the gospel's proclamation. In their proclamation of Jesus' victory over sin at the cross, early preachers spoke of God's victory over death. The death and resurrection of Jesus are the basis of the gospel from the first century to this day.

The wounded living body of Jesus is compelling evidence for the resurrection. Jesus' appearances launched a community of believers who received the Third Person of the Trinity, the Holy Spirit. The evidence for their encounter with an invisible God was in the ordinary speaking of all the known languages of the world even though they didn't know them the day before. Following this mass proclamation of the gospel, people asked, "What does this

7. John 11:38–44; 12:2.

mean?"[8] That is, the anthropology of unlearned yet spoken languages prompted a theological question. The rest of Christianity is a historical account of how that question was answered, beginning with Peter, right up to last Sunday. Just as the living human being Jesus of Nazareth appeared to Mary Magdalene, two people walking home, fearful disciples, and a reluctant Thomas, who believed only after he touched the wounds of Jesus, another form of Jesus Christ appeared on earth; that is, the church. The best evidence of Christ's resurrection is the living body of Christ, the church, gathered for celebration and scattered in mission.

It is the wounded yet forgiven church which replaces Jesus on earth to continue his ministry of healing and forgiveness of sin and sinners. The body of Christ continues to prove its "resurrection" from the death of sin by doing mundane eating and drinking during a most sacred ritual—the Eucharist. By eating the body of Christ and drinking his blood, the church continues to proclaim his victory over sin—the theological meaning of his cross. By existing as an alive community of believing human beings, the church continues to proclaim Christ's resurrection; that is, his victory over death. Just as the crucified-resurrected body of Jesus Christ launched the gospel, the cruciform-living church perpetuates the message of "Christ crucified" fueled by the Holy Spirit's power derived from "Christ resurrected." A crucified-resurrected Christ exists on earth today as his church. One might even say, the church is an incarnation of the incarnation. It begins as an infant and, like Jesus, grows in the knowledge and grace of the Father. Given this brief interpretation of the resurrection of Jesus Christ from the biblical witness, we now turn our attention to Bonhoeffer's theology of the resurrection.

Bonhoeffer's Theology of the Resurrection

Among his final letters from prison, Dietrich Bonhoeffer called for nonreligious vocabulary to express biblical concepts. In this

8. Acts 2:12.

section we will explore his theology of the resurrection and how it might be communicated in ordinary language, beginning with his anthropological insights.

Bonhoeffer's anthropology of the resurrection informs how he thinks about the meaning of God's raising Jesus of Nazareth from the dead. He begins with the human body of Jesus Christ. His theology of the resurrection is embedded in the incarnation: the Word became flesh. Far from his thinking is some spiritual resurrection of a celestial being. Thomas believed only after he touched the physical wounds on Jesus' hands and side. The human body of Jesus is the human body of Adam without sin. But as Bonhoeffer says, "The human body of Jesus became the resurrected body and the body of Adam became the body of Christ."[9] Of course, he has in mind here Paul's equation of the body of Christ to the church. A key question is this: How does an egocentric body of Adam become the resurrected body of Jesus Christ? Bonhoeffer states that the body of Adam has to be broken in order for the body of resurrection, the body of Christ, to be created. It is the cross which accomplishes such a breaking in its victory over the sin conveyed through Adam's body and the resurrection which ushers in God's victory over death. Bonhoeffer's view of the resurrection evolves from a created human being, a manger, and a cross. This book simply attempts to echo his anthropology as a method to arrive at a theology more robust than one communicated using in-house cliché understood only by those with a religious background.

Vicarious representative action is the key concept in Bonhoeffer's theology. Jesus Christ becomes our advocate in our place on our behalf both on a cross and out of a tomb. The new, yet mysterious, crucified-resurrected body of Jesus is the basis for a new humanity, "a humanity-in-Adam is transformed into humanity-in-Christ."[10] That new humanity is the church. Note the absence of the word *spiritual* in Bonhoeffer's vocabulary. Bonhoeffer's theology is not spiritual but incarnational. His view of the resurrection is incarnational, not mystical. It is the *body* of Jesus Christ that

9. Bonhoeffer, *Sanctorum Communio*, 147.
10. Ibid.

God raises from the dead. His reason is that there is nothing about spirituality which makes Christ necessary. Virtually every non-Christian religion has its spirituality. Incarnation requires that one speak of God in human form. In fact, the acid test for authentic Christian spirituality is its acknowledgment that the Second Person of the Trinity became human. The resurrected body of Jesus digested broiled fish.

Bonhoeffer speaks collaboratively of the resurrection, the church, and the Holy Spirit. Referring to the church as a community-of-the-cross, he says: "A community-of-the-cross exists only through the Easter message."[11] Here he speaks of a partnership between the church and the resurrection. In his letter to the Ephesian Christians, Paul speaks of the cross as dismantling all dividing walls between human beings, beginning with Jews and Gentiles creating one new humanity, the church. A key to Bonhoeffer's grasp of the resurrection is how it influences human community. When he speaks of human community, he is speaking of the church. Bonhoeffer cannot talk about the church without mentioning the Holy Spirit. *"The church originates with the out-pouring of the Holy Spirit, and so too the Holy Spirit is the spirit of the church-community of Christ."*[12] Bonhoeffer is quick to point out that the church is a nonreligious community. By that he means that the church is a living community of faith, not a disconnected aggregate of like-mined individuals.

Nor does he say that the church is a spiritual community. It is precisely Bonhoeffer's anthropology of the resurrection, his insistence on Jesus' human body becoming the resurrected body of Adam that defines the church. The church is a restored human community. He cannot speak of the resurrection, the church, or the Holy Spirit without implying the other. It's like speaking of the community of the Father, Son, and Holy Spirit; each one implies the other two. The collaborative nature of the Trinity models how an integration of resurrection, church, and Holy Spirit results in a new holistic humanity unified across all cultures, languages, and ethnicities.

11. Ibid., 151.

12. Ibid., 132, italics in original.

Participation is a key word in Bonhoeffer's theology. He speaks of participating in the sufferings of Christ for the world. When speaking of a participation in the resurrection, Bonhoeffer begins with the incarnation. "Only the person taken on in Christ is the real human being; only the person confronted by the cross of Christ is the judged human being; only the person who participates in the resurrection of Christ is the renewed human being."[13] Note his progression from incarnation to redemption to resurrection. His phrase "the person taken on in Christ" refers to the incarnation. He never speaks of some religiously pious person when he talks about participating in Christ's resurrection. It is a renewed human being, energized by the Holy Spirit, who participates in the church-community.

Speaking of a worldly Christianity, Bonhoeffer states: "The Christian is not a religious person but simply a human being in the same way Jesus was a human being."[14] His worldly Christianity is not to be thought of negatively. *Worldly* is a positive term in his theology. It is rooted in the incarnation. It challenges a self-centered inward religiosity. It urges a down-to-earth faith channeled into a this-worldly concern for humanity. Bonhoeffer's thoughts about becoming human require more than any perfunctory religious commitment to tradition. His notion of being human within a year of his death (1944) echoes his first academic dissertation, *Sanctorum Communio* (1927). A human church characterized his theology throughout his life. The authentic human being follows Jesus in his incarnation, crucifixion, and resurrection. As a renewed community of the cross, the church is to participate in the being of Jesus. He states that faith is participating in the being of Jesus. While this may sound abstract, Bonhoeffer insists that such participation in the resurrection means getting involved in the concrete ordinary tasks of life for the betterment of the neighbor near and far. Here he "resurrects" Luther. As the sanctuary is constructed in the middle of the village, Christ exists at the center of life for all humanity.

13. Bonhoeffer, *Ethics*, 134.
14. Bonhoeffer, *Letters and Papers from Prison*, 485.

Finally, Bonhoeffer's theology of the resurrection concentrates on how Christians live their life on earth without speculating about what life might be like in heaven. While clearly acknowledging the resurrection as God's victory over death he says: "The Christian hope of the resurrection refers people to their life on earth."[15] He prefers to speak of redemption and resurrection within history and prior to death. The church is a community of persons evolving from humanity in Adam to humanity in Christ by "coming back to earth" as renewed people of God. Bonhoeffer thinks of resurrection as an experience in *this* life. The church as the resurrected body of Christ replaces the historic body of Jesus as the new humanity on earth. One might even call it a re-incarnation of God on earth where the church in Christ's absence now becomes the vicarious representative for others in its ministry of reconciliation.

In sum, Bonhoeffer's theology of the resurrection begins with a vocabulary based in anthropology. Taking its trajectory from the incarnation, he speaks of the transformation of the human body of Adam into the resurrected body of Jesus Christ. His view of the resurrection is incarnational, not spiritual. Bonhoeffer speaks collaboratively of the resurrection, the church, and the Holy Spirit with Jesus as the vicarious representative. The resurrection for Bonhoeffer is not static, but a dynamic participation in a new life for others both within the church and for the neighbor near and far.

Conclusion

This chapter has presented a theology of Jesus Christ's resurrection as victory over death. We explored several texts from the Scripture offering various nuances for thinking and speaking of God's raising Jesus back to life. First, we considered Jesus' own words about his coming resurrection; then we noted how others spoke of the possibility that he'd rise from the dead; and finally analyzed how the pristine church proclaimed the resurrection. From the biblical witness we then assembled and assessed several aspects of the

15. Ibid., 447.

resurrection based upon the premise that good theology comes from good anthropology. This chapter provided a look into Bonhoeffer's writings from his dissertation to his last letters as a basis for his theology of the resurrection. We took special note of his use of the human body, preferring an incarnational perspective of the resurrection. Finally, we saw how he believes the resurrection, the church, and the Holy Spirit work collaboratively. With this chapter we close all new information about how an anthropology of a community of people informs a theology of the church. The final chapter summarizes the book.

Conclusion

THE CHURCH DOESN'T NEED to be more spiritual, but more incarnational. We introduced this book with the statement: "Good anthropology makes for good theology." We took Dietrich Bonhoeffer as our conversation partner, who urged the church to communicate biblical concepts in nonreligious language. Rather than beginning with lofty theology, Bonhoeffer looked at culture "from below"; only then did he interpret what he saw theologically. We've adopted his method, beginning with an anthropology of the church's rituals and symbols followed by a theological interpretation.

Dividing the book into two parts—part 1: Anthropology, and part 2: Theology—we viewed the church as an ethnographic object using the same categories that an anthropologist would use to study a people group. By observing the church's rituals during Advent, Lent, and Easter, we discovered key symbols of the Christian faith: manger, bread, wine, cross, and tomb, respectively. Each symbol is a mundane object. Each term, incarnation, redemption, and resurrection, derives from a theological interpretation of its respective symbol.

We assigned theological meaning to each symbol as derived from both the observed and narrative behavior of persons in worship or from the biblical witness, respectively. Bonhoeffer's theology of the church, incarnation, cross, and resurrection informed and enriched our interpretation of the symbols.

To speak nonreligiously of the church is to view it as a community of recovering human beings. It is not to reduce God to a problem-solver, but to follow him when all problems are solved and all questions are answered. The message of the church focuses upon the center of human existence, not its periphery. Jesus Christ is the center of all human existence.

To think nonreligiously of the incarnation is to speak of the scandal of God in a feeding trough for oxen. The baby in the manger was the holy Trinity. A mysterious Holy Spirit got Mary pregnant. Jesus, the Son of God, was a Jewish boy. The scandal of Jesus' birth continued as a teenage girl had to convince her mother and father that Joseph was not her baby's father. A twelve-year-old stumped the synagogue teachers and elders who were convinced that Joseph was Jesus' father. No doubt, Joseph had an identity crisis related to his fatherhood, especially when his son spoke of "being about his father's business" without talking about carpentry. Bonhoeffer reminds us that it is *God* in the manger. That God became human affirms his love for human beings. The best the church can be is human just like Jesus was during his ministry on earth. Like Jesus, the church is incognito. It is not what it appears to be—just another gathering of people. The human church is a community of persons filled with the Holy Spirit who appear to be only human. Jesus stated that his church would do even greater things than he did. The miracle of the church is that while masked as just ordinary persons, we are living sacraments doing the gospel for others as God gives us power, grace, and strength.

The cross is a scandalous symbol for the gospel. It is the unlikely location for humanity's healing. Bread and wine are sacraments; that is, mundane objects assigned sacred value. Bread symbolizes the broken human body of Jesus; wine, the crushing experience of his bleeding because of nails and a spear. There is nothing religious about the cross. God simply does not belong on a Roman cross! Theologically, without it no one would be redeemed. It is not a symbol of defeat. Jesus' death means victory over sin. The cross is a symbol of victory! The work of the Second Person of the Trinity, the Son, on the cross accomplished victory over the power and penalty for sin. The cross is a symbol of grace and mercy! Bonhoeffer's view of Jesus Christ was as our substitute once for all yet our continual advocate forever. The church, the body of Christ, is the scandalous replacement of God on earth as a vicarious community for others.

An empty tomb does not prove the resurrection. The reappearance of Jesus of Nazareth does. The mysteriously crucified-resurrected human body of Jesus launched the Christian church. No sermon in the New Testament proclaims an empty tomb as a reason to have faith in Jesus Christ. The Apostle Paul stated the gospel message as "Christ Crucified" empowered by "He is risen! He is risen indeed!" Without the resurrection, preaching has no power. Without the cross, there is no message. Bonhoeffer stated that Jesus Christ's uniquely resurrected body guarantees that all humanity will rise from the dead to final judgment. The resurrection is God's victory over death for all human beings. Belief in Christ's resurrection removes any fear of death. For the Christian, death is a path leading to eternal presence with God. The church, resurrection, and Holy Spirit all work together as God's victory over death. While no one comes back from death, in a way every Christian comes back to earth as a new person *within history prior to death*. It's what Jesus means by being born again. The Christian is a different person from what she was before knowing Christ, even though she looks the same. The Christian is a different person by virtue of being possessed by the Holy Spirit. That changes everything!

One's relationship with God is personal, but never lonely confined only to one's individual faith. The normal Christian life is lived in community with other pilgrims who are on the same journey. That community is not pious, religious, or even spiritual. It is incarnational. Such a community may be called a *human church*.

Bibliography

Alexander, Robert, and James Donaldson, eds. *The Ante-Nicene Fathers*. Grand Rapids: Eerdmans, 1980.

Angelou, Maya. "The Caged Bird." https://www.poetryfoundation.org/poems/48989/caged-bird.

———. *I Know Why the Caged Bird Sings*. London: Virago, 2012.

Apostolos-Cappadona, Diane. *Dictionary of Christian Art*. New York: Continuum, 1994.

Barker, Kenneth, et al., eds. *The New International Version Study Bible*. Grand Rapids: Zondervan, 1985.

Barnhart, Robert K., ed. *The Barnhart Concise Dictionary of Etymology*. New York: HarperCollins, 1995.

Bischoff, Paul O. *The Secular Church*. Wheaton, IL: self-published, 2015.

Bonhoeffer, Dietrich. *Act and Being*. Edited by Wayne W. Floyd. Minneapolis: Fortress, 1996.

———. *Creation and Fall*. Edited by John W. de Gruchy. Minneapolis: Fortress, 1996.

———. *Discipleship*. Edited by Geffrey B. Kelly and John D. Godsey. Minneapolis: Fortress, 1996.

———. *Ethics*. Edited Clifford J. Green. Minneapolis: Fortress, 2005.

———. *God Is in the Manger: Reflections on Advent and Christmas*. Edited by Jana Reiss. Louisville: Westminster John Knox, 2011.

———. *Letters and Papers from Prison*. Edited John W. de Gruchy. Minneapolis: Fortress, 2010.

———. *Life Together; Prayerbook of the Bible*. Edited by Geffrey B. Kelly. Minneapolis: Fortress, 1996.

———. *Sanctorum Communio*. Edited Clifford J. Green. Minneapolis: Fortress, 1998.

Cannell, Fenella. *The Anthropology of Christianity*. Raleigh-Durham: Duke University Press, 2006.

Craig, William Lane. "The Guard at the Tomb." In *New Testament Studies* 1 (1984) 1588.

Craigie, Peter C. *The Book of Deuteronomy*. Grand Rapids: Eerdmans, 1974.

BIBLIOGRAPHY

Douglas, J. D., ed. *The New Greek-English Interlinear New Testament*. Translated by R. K. Brown and P. W. Comfort. Wheaton: Tyndale, 1990.

Duchesne, Louis. *Christian Worship*. New York: Macmillan, 1919.

Elwell, Walter A., ed. *The Evangelical Dictionary of Theology*. Grand Rapids: Baker, 2001.

Hengel, M. *Crucifixion in the Ancient World and the Folly of the Message of the Cross*. Philadelphia: Fortress, 1977.

Josephus, Flavius. "Against Apion." earlyjewishwritings.com/text/josephus/apion1.html.

Larsen, Timothy. *The Slain God: Anthropologists and the Christian Faith*. Oxford: Oxford University Press, 2016.

Menachemson, Nolan. "A Brief History of Jewish Burial." http://www.avotaynu.com/books/Chapter1a.pdf.

Peucker, Paul. "The Easter Sunrise Service." *This Month in Moravian History*, April 2007.

Vander Zee, Leonard J. *Christ, Baptism and the Lord's Supper*. Downers Grove: Intervarsity, 2004.

Whitehead, Tony L. "Basic Classical Ethnological Research Methods." *Cultural Ecology of Health and Change* 3 (2004) 7–14.

Whiteman, Darrell L. "Part II: Anthropology and Mission: The Incarnational Connection." *International Journal of Frontier Missions* 21 (2004) 4–15.

Wiberg, Glen V. *The Covenant Book of Worship*. Chicago: Covenant, 1981.

Williams, Frank. "Adversus Haereses." In *The Panarion of Epiphanius of Salamis*, book 2. Leiden, Netherlands: Brill, 1994.